"You are not alone, and it is possible to reconnect with who and what is most important to you. This is the hope-filled message of *The Moral Injury Workbook*. Whether you have done or failed to do something, or something has been done to you, if you have experienced a betrayal of moral values you hold dear, this workbook offers evidence-based strategies for how to move forward and reclaim your life. It is an inspiring and essential resource for anyone facing the complex, painful, and often hidden struggles that result from moral injury."

—**Jenna LeJeune, PhD**, licensed clinical psychologist; president of
Portland Psychotherapy Clinic, Research, and Training Center;
and coauthor of *Values in Therapy*

"Providing essential resources for both therapists and clients, this book is a comprehensive and compassionate account of finding a way forward after surviving a range of adverse experiences. Based on science and grounded in the heart, the authors have delivered a text that combines clinical insights, personal stories, and useful exercises for finding meaning in living. This book is essential reading for anyone interested in trauma and moral injury. Both clients and therapists will find support and comfort in these words, which give a sense of purpose to doing the difficult work of addressing moral injury."

—**Victoria Follette, PhD, PsyD**, program chair, director of clinical training,
and professor in the school of psychology at Florida Institute of Technology

"If you find yourself haunted by a past event where you hurt or injured someone, or witnessed this happening to someone else, then I urge you to consider this book. The authors relate powerful stories and tools that can help you move from alienation and disconnection to repair and wholeness. If your moral sense has been disrupted or damaged, this book is a lifeline."

—**Jason B. Luoma, PhD**, shame and self-compassion researcher,
and coauthor of *Learning ACT* and *Values in Therapy*

"Grounded in the collective clinical and scientific expertise of the four authors, this important contribution is full of compassionate, wise, and much-needed, practical tools for addressing moral injury with acceptance and commitment therapy (ACT). For persons seeking to heal their lives from the wounds of morally injurious events, they will find a treasure trove of insights and strategies for restoring human connection and meaningful living. For clinicians and trainees who desire to incorporate ACT in their attempts to address moral injury in therapeutic settings, this book is similarly essential reading, and one that will be reviewed again and again."

—**Joseph Currier, PhD**, associate professor of psychology at the University of South Alabama, and lead editor of *Addressing Moral Injury in Clinical Practice*

"This useful resource for anyone suffering from or caring for those with moral injury helpfully brings ACT principles to bear in a manner that invites a fresh, honest, and ultimately hopeful exploration of one's moral identity."

—**Jason Nieuwsma, PhD**, associate director of the VA Mid-Atlantic MIRECC Mental Health and Chaplaincy program, and associate professor at Duke University Medical Center

The
Moral Injury
Workbook

ACCEPTANCE & COMMITMENT THERAPY SKILLS *for* MOVING BEYOND SHAME, ANGER & TRAUMA *to* RECLAIM YOUR VALUES

WYATT R. EVANS, PhD
ROBYN D. WALSER, PhD
KENT D. DRESCHER, PhD
JACOB K. FARNSWORTH, PhD

New Harbinger Publications, Inc.

Publisher's Note

This publication is designed to provide accurate and authoritative information in regard to the subject matter covered. It is sold with the understanding that the publisher is not engaged in rendering psychological, financial, legal, or other professional services. If expert assistance or counseling is needed, the services of a competent professional should be sought.

Distributed in Canada by Raincoast Books

Copyright © 2020 by Wyatt R. Evans, Robyn D. Walser, Kent D. Drescher, and Jacob K. Farnsworth
New Harbinger Publications, Inc.
5674 Shattuck Avenue
Oakland, CA 94609
www.newharbinger.com

Cover design by Amy Shoup

Acquired by Tesilya Hanauer

Edited by Kristi Hein

Library of Congress Cataloging-in-Publication Data on file

Printed in the United States of America

22   21   20

10   9   8   7   6   5   4   3   2   1   First Printing

We dedicate this book to the veterans and service members who have served their country and, in so doing, sacrificed and suffered. We are especially grateful to those who shared their stories and pain with us in developing acceptance and commitment therapy (ACT) for moral healing and teaching us about moral challenges and dilemmas, including those that arise during times of war. We are deeply inspired by their humanity and their desire to return to their values. Without their willingness and bravery to reveal their innermost sorrow, we could not have begun our journey of understanding moral injury, and its function and fallout. Their persistence has assisted us in developing ACT as a path to recovery. They have shared their hopes that through their pain, others' lives might be improved. This book is inspired by that hope and is the direct result of their openness and desire to offer healing.

Contents

Acknowledgments

We want to thank our friends and colleagues, Dr. Lauren Borges and Dr. Sean Barnes. Our collaborations with them have been essential in both developing the science of ACT as an intervention for moral injury and cultivating a path to healing for those who suffer with the same. In our deep appreciation for their dedication to the science of and recovery from moral injury, we consider them part of our authorship team. We want to acknowledge their continuing efforts to bring science-based and compassionate recovery to those who are on a journey of rediscovering values in the midst of moral pain.

—WRE, RDW, KDD, and JKF

To my husband, Michael, for his love and patient support, and to my parents, for their unending encouragement.

—WRE

To my mom, who as always is my hero, and to Bobby and Deon, for their great service and dedication; thank you for doing what you do and being a wonderful support to me.

—RDW

To my amazing family, who provide love, encouragement, and joy every day: my wife, Susan, our sons and their wives, and my grandchildren, who provide a lens to see my world with eyes of hope and joy.

—KDD

To my wife, Joanna, and our four beautiful children, who together are my greatest moral good.

—JKF

Acknowledgments

Introduction

Freedom, morality, and the human dignity of the individual consists precisely in this: that he does good not because he is forced to do so, but because he freely conceives it...

—Mikhail Bakunin

You are not alone. Though it may seem that way in the aftermath of situations in which you or others made decisions that led to immensely hurtful outcomes, you are not alone in that pain, and you will not be alone on your healing journey. In reading this book, you'll be joined by an incredibly diverse group of people. People who have faced seemingly impossible choices. People who have caused great harm, as well as those who have been harmed greatly. People who have witnessed atrocities and violence. People who have been betrayed, and those whose past behaviors involved betrayal. You may also be joined by therapists, counselors, chaplains, and others who seek to bring healing to those who suffer from the fallout of moral pain. You, they, and we are all connected by pain, and we are all now on this healing journey together.

If you are wondering whether moral injury is an accurate label for your experience (or the experience of someone you care about), first consider what led you to open this book and also know that we will take time to define moral injury and how it grows from moral pain. We will also explore what kinds of events lead to moral injury. It may help you to know that moral injury is not a new experience in the world. Philosophers and theologians have been writing about it for ages, and humans have been struggling with it for much longer than that. We hope that as you read this book and work through its exercises, you will come to more fully understand moral injury, its impact, and how to recover from it.

Moral Dilemmas Across Time

The human race has long been involved in moral dilemmas. Across time we have endured tests of survival—protection of ourselves and our families, communities, and countries. As we have solved problems and adapted to changes and challenges, we have tried to secure our futures and control outcomes linked to how we live, our freedoms and rights, and how to maintain personal and loving connections to those who mean the most to us. There are moral elements in all of these aspects of our survival and our relationships.

From the times when early human tribes competed for scarce resources to the moral dilemmas presented by modern activity, such as global warming and internet privacy, humans have faced questions of right and wrong. Sometimes it seems very clear what is morally right; at other times, it's hard to know the answer. This is especially so when the stakes are high, such as when we go through a traumatic experience or struggle with competing and complex values.

It's not always easy to know when and how to act when we face one of these moral dilemmas. Indeed, this is what makes it a dilemma. And some moral violations that happen in one setting may not be a violation in other settings. Moral violations can occur under terrible circumstances, such as war or natural disasters. They can happen by accident or during a momentary lapse in judgment. They can happen as people act out of power and greed. So moral injury is complex, both in how it happens and in its aftermath. Whatever the circumstances were that caused your moral injury, this book offers hope. There is a way forward to moral healing, and we believe what you find here will help you in that journey.

A New Perspective on Morality, Pain, and Suffering

The complexity of human morality is a unique feature of our species. Humans have developed systems of rules, punishments, rewards, and social norms for ethical behavior far beyond what any other species has developed. So it shouldn't be surprising that, when we experience a highly stressful life event that forces us to choose between right and wrong, we may struggle with moral questions, doubts, and pain. We may have to make split-second decisions, take action in the face of war and natural disasters, or respond instantly to an accident.

Traumatic experiences like these can lead us to question our moral worldviews or our understanding of who we are as a person. They can unravel our personal sense of self, deeply affecting how we see ourselves, others, and our places in the world. When your deepest values are violated in high-stakes circumstances, you may question your faith, your own moral truths, and what you stand for in life. We wrote this book to help you and others like you—who suffer, trapped in moral pain—to restore your hope and sense of yourself as whole, and to return to a life that is true to your values.

Morality Up Front: A Capacity of Both Mind and Heart

As we begin this journey, we want to share with you some key aspects of morality up front. This will assist you as you read, because in most chapters we'll be exploring morality of the mind and heart.

Evolutionary psychologists tell us that human morality evolved as a way of keeping social communities intact and thriving. Our morality discourages us from cheating, deceiving, or injuring others or acting in ways that would harm the group or place the community at risk. We humans have evolved and thrived through our capacity to cooperate and act in the service of each other as well as of ourselves. This capacity is so crucial that humans have not one, but two parallel moral systems that, together, make up our personal morality and influence our moral actions and reactions in daily life. In this book, we'll call these the *morality of the mind* and the *morality of the heart.*

Morality of the Mind

Morality of the mind concerns mostly what we all learn—that is, what we're taught. As we learn, we become thinking, imagining beings—we develop our minds. So the *morality of the mind* is shorthand for all of our thinking and talking about morality.

As we grow and develop through childhood, we learn principles and ideals about what is right and wrong from our families, culture, religion, and legal system. We learn these things through instruction and by watching the examples of others. Indeed, our learning history forms our core beliefs and values. Most people's ability to engage moral thinking and reasoning about right and wrong develops at a fairly young age and becomes more sophisticated over time.

Morality of the Heart

The second type of morality, a morality of the heart, refers to emotional experience— that is, what we feel rather than think. This can include bodily sensations that accompany our emotions. These are the "gut" reactions we feel—instant experiences of sensation and emotion. Often we feel both types of moral responses at the same time—a combination we can think of as *moral intuitions*. These emotionally charged reactions about right and wrong emerge spontaneously in a situation, too quickly to have come from logical reasoning or memory—that is, through mental processes alone (Haidt, 2001). Moral intuitions seem to be quite universal—they're found in societies all over the world.

Dr. Jonathan Haidt and his colleagues identified at least five types of situations that seem to evoke strong emotionally based moral reactions across cultures:

- Harm inflicted on others, especially the weak and vulnerable

- Unfairness and injustice

- Disloyalty or betrayal of one's family, community, or country

- Disrespect for leadership and authority

- Desecration of or disrespect for ideals or things viewed as sacred

We'll talk more about these types of situations when we talk about morally injurious events in the coming chapters.

While the intensity of reactions varies across individuals, groups, and cultures, people exposed to these situations will experience reactions based on a gut feeling or immediate emotional response. They will immediately intuit right and wrong as a felt sense—as a rapid emotional reaction happening as just described. This is the morality of the heart.

Mind and Heart in Conflict

Quite often, morality of the mind and heart will be in sync. What you think and feel in a situation line up together without conflict. However, sometimes these two moral systems can be out of sync. Sometimes our mind tells us an action is right while the heart says that it's wrong, or vice versa; for example, offering help to someone who has done terrible things to people, leaving people behind in life-and-death situations, or agreeing to the withdrawal of medical intervention for someone who is suffering without hope of recovery. In instances such as these, we may experience a moral dilemma.

Throughout this book, we'll share many stories of people who have experienced deeply painful situations that involved a violation of a core moral value. These stories are meant to illustrate the painful consequences of such violations and to guide your growing understanding of moral injury and moral healing. Many of the stories will also illustrate how mind and heart can come into conflict. Let's take a look at one story now, to introduce you to a recurring character in this book and to give you a more concrete example of the kind of moral conflict that our minds and hearts can endure.

• *The Story of the Sergeant and Humankind*

It's 2009, and Sergeant (SGT) Howell and his unit have been deployed to Afghanistan as part of the U.S. surge to push back the Taliban and reinforce Afghan security forces. It's another unbearably hot day, and SGT Howell and his unit are at a vehicle checkpoint outside a city known to be a hub of Taliban activity. Suddenly, one of SGT Howell's soldiers shouts that he sees a child walking toward the checkpoint. After another minute a soldier in the unit shouts, "It's Abdul!"—the ten-year-old son of a local Afghan man paid to work on the U.S. base.

Abdul had come to idolize SGT Howell and his soldiers over the last eight months. Raising his scope to his eye, SGT Howell can see that Abdul is looking down and that his shirt seems to be strangely padded and oversized. With a dawning realization, SGT Howell sees that under the shirt of the young boy is an improvised explosive device. SGT Howell shouts to his team, "He's got a vest! He's got a vest!"

In an instant, each of the soldiers train their weapons on the approaching boy as SGT Howell yells at Abdul to stop and stay where he is so that they can attempt to disarm the bomb. Instead of stopping, however, Abdul raises his head as he continues to walk, revealing a face in anguish and wet with streaming tears. SGT Howell knows that the closer Abdul comes, the deadlier the vest's blast will be to his unit. A horrible sinking sensation sweeps over him. Without another word, SGT Howell picks up his weapon and takes aim. For one second, before he slowly squeezes the trigger, SGT Howell can see, framed in his crosshairs, the crying, terrified face of Abdul.

As a reader, pause and reflect on what you are experiencing right now. What do you feel, and what thoughts come up for you? For many, the experience of SGT Howell will feel disturbing and unresolved. You might realize, on one level, that SGT Howell had few options to choose from; at the same time, you might recoil or feel angry at the taking of Abdul's life. Some readers may even feel gratitude to members of the armed forces for shouldering the burden of these excruciatingly difficult decisions. And though each of these reactions would be reasonable, it would be a mistake to conclude that moral dilemmas like this happen only in extreme environments like a war zone. Whether we notice them or not, these dilemmas are happening today, everywhere: where we work, or learn, or shop; in our streets; and in our homes. Whether you recognize it or not, this is not just a story about Abdul and SGT Howell. It is also a story about us, and it's a story about you.

Roadmap for This Book

There are three parts to this book. The first provides important information on the types of traumatic and hurtful experiences that can lead to moral pain. Exercises in this section will help you take the important first step of understanding where and when your suffering first began. From there, you'll build your awareness of the different types of moral pain as well as an understanding of the purposes of this kind of pain. Next we'll share a new—possibly surprising to you—way of thinking about how our moral pain can turn into the moral suffering known as *moral injury*. This will be a key piece of information to keep in mind as you read. We'll then briefly introduce the healing processes of acceptance and commitment therapy (ACT) that will make up the rest of the book. Before leaving part 1, you'll explore your moral communities. As you read on, you will learn that moral wounds are social wounds. This means that, to repair the social wound of moral injury, it's essential to increase your awareness of your own social groups and connections.

Each of the five chapters in part 2 is centered around one of the healing processes of ACT. In these chapters, you'll learn about and, most importantly, *practice* engaging these skills to

- Broaden your sense of self

- Gain some distance from the stories in which you've been stuck

- Connect or reconnect with your values

- Increase your willingness to have and even embrace pain in the service of your values

- Engage with your values in the present moment

Part 1 has set the foundation from which you will begin your healing journey; part 2 helps you determine the direction in which you will go as well as builds and strengthens the essential tools for your journey.

Finally, part 3 introduces two processes—forgiveness and compassion—that many readers will find relevant to their journey. These may appear challenging, but you will see that they are essential tools necessary for healing and growth. Again, exercises and personal exploration activities will help you understand what role these two processes will play in your overall healing process. The final chapter is about putting everything you've learned into action. Healing, thriving, and, in fact, living are about *doing*. This final chapter will invite, encourage, and guide you to take committed actions to live out the values you've identified and explored throughout the book.

Not Everything Will Fit for Everyone

As you progress through the book, you'll come across many stories, exercises, and explanations. Some won't resonate with you, and that's to be expected. You'll find others you can relate to on a very deep personal level. Each reader who picks up this book will likely find value and meaning in a different set of stories, skills, and exercises.

The events that can cause moral injury take many forms. Some readers may have been harmed by someone else. Some readers have caused harm to others. And others may not have caused harm or been harmed, but witnessed the harm being inflicted, powerless or afraid to intervene. The emotions that moral injury may entail include shame, guilt, contempt, disgust, and/or anger. These emotions and your judgments or evaluations may be directed at you, another person or group of people, humanity as a whole, or God. Each possibility and any combination can be a part of moral injury.

To get the most out of this book, we ask that you explore each new idea and each activity with openness and curiosity. In doing so, you will allow those pieces that are most relevant to your own healing to solidify and become part of your journey. And the pieces that may not be a part of your unique healing process? Review them and let them pass by without hindering your progress.

Each Chapter Is a Piece of a Puzzle

We encourage you to move through this book in order, carefully exploring the content of each chapter. In ACT, each process works with the others to enable healing, growth, and vital living. In the same way, each chapter of this book works with the others. Each is a piece of a puzzle. Each is important on its own; putting them together creates the complete picture of moral healing. Some chapters may feel less important to you, a smaller piece of the puzzle; others will seem to be more important, larger pieces. But without all the pieces, the picture is less clear.

Seek Support and Create (or Recreate) Connections

Remember us saying that moral wounds are social wounds? Morality keeps communities together and guides our actions toward others. When someone violates that morality—whether it's you or anyone else—that creates a rift, a disconnect between you and your community—family, friends, faith communities, and so on. As we'll describe at length in part 1, if moral injury is about disconnection, moral healing is about (re)connection.

You may or may not have shared your morally injurious experiences with another person or other people. Likewise, you may or may not have shared your reactions—your thoughts and feelings—with others. Either way, it is okay. When, how, and with whom you connect is your choice. We're not going to tell you at any point in this book what you *should* do. Rather, we'll explore options and leave it up to you. We respect your choices.

Where the work you're about to do highlights places of disconnection, we invite you to consider how you might reconnect or form new connections. Whether you connect with a loved one, a battle buddy, a religious or spiritual leader, or simply one more caring human being, connecting to others is a central part of moral healing. How much of this work you share with them is up to you. There are many values-based ways to connect, and we'll explore several of those in this book.

Use the Workbook on Your Own or Alongside Your Therapy

We wrote this workbook specifically for readers of all backgrounds who are suffering under the weight of moral injury. You don't need to be working with a therapist or counselor to use it. If you are working with a therapist and want to complete the work you've begun by picking up this book, then ask your therapist about possibly working through this book together. Working with a therapist can really help move you through painful experiences toward vital living. And if you happen to be a therapist or counselor yourself, consider sharing this book with your clients if they are struggling with moral pain and experiencing moral injury.

The Gravity of Moral Injury Can't Always Be Captured in Writing

The suffering of moral injury can be immense. The events that can lead to moral injury are some of the most difficult known to humans—killing, sexual assault, betrayal, and failing to prevent these sorts of tragedies—and often words simply cannot express the depth of pain and suffering experienced in the aftermath. Each of us, the authors, has witnessed this anguish and despair and sought to ease it in the people we have worked with in therapy. But it's hard to capture in ink on the pages of a book. We hope that, as you read the words here, you'll recognize this challenge and let the work in this book connect with the suffering you feel that cannot be captured by words—but that can be healed by the processes we'll explore together.

Our Hope for You

If you've picked up this book, you know pain. You are human, and pain is a crucial, albeit uncomfortable, part of our experience on this earth. It is also likely that you picked up this book because you also know suffering—your own, a loved one's, or a client's. We hope that this book will serve as a guide to help alleviate that suffering. We cannot eliminate pain. Even if we could, we would not want to. Does that sound strange? What could we mean? We hope this question sparks your curiosity as you begin this journey.

Most of all, we hope that, even with pain, the work you've begun by picking up this book will reconnect you with your deepest values—even, perhaps especially, the values that have been violated. In the same way, we hope this work will enable both reconnection and new connections to others. May this be the start of a new part of your life journey—one about living fully, here and now, committed to acting on your values rather than reacting to pain and suffering.

PART 1

Preparing for the Journey of Healing

CHAPTER 1

The Pain of Violated Values

When your values are clear to you, making decisions becomes easier.

—Roy E. Disney

Robert is a forty-three-year-old father of two. Last year, his wife was diagnosed with an aggressive form of cancer, and she had to stop working while undergoing treatment. The loss of her income and additional medical costs put a burden on the family finances. To support his wife and children, Robert took a second job. He worked long hours, including night shifts. One morning he arrived home completely exhausted. His wife had just finished getting the kids ready but was feeling too fatigued and ill to drive them to school. Robert encouraged her to rest; he would drop them off.

Running late, Robert finally got the kids out the front door. He was normally even-tempered, but in his frustration he yelled angrily, "Hurry up! Get in the car!" The kids were surprised by this outburst and became quiet, quickly taking their seats. Robert regretted his anger, but feeling relief that the kids were cooperating, he started driving. In the silence, Robert fought his exhaustion. He rolled the car windows down, hoping the fresh air would keep him awake. At that moment, a text alert chimed on his phone. Robert didn't usually text while driving, but he looked down and tapped the phone. As he did, his car passed through a red light. An oncoming SUV struck Robert's car.

Hours later, Robert learned the full impact of the accident. When the children had climbed into their seats, with the tension of Robert's yelling, his son had forgotten to buckle his seat belt. In his exhaustion, Robert had also forgotten to check whether they were both buckled in. In the collision, his son had been thrown out of the car. He did not survive the accident.

As you read Robert's story, imagine the intense mental and emotional pain he experienced as he realized the severity of the accident and its consequences. He might feel, in addition to the anguish of loss, self-blame, shame, regret, and doubts or judgments about himself as a father. Realizing that his actions—forgetting to check the seat belts, glancing down at the incoming text message—contributed to the tragedy will likely lead to intense pain and struggle. His guilt and self-blame arise from a violation of his most deeply held values: love for and protection of his family. Robert has experienced a morally injurious event.

Defining Morally Injurious Events

A *morally injurious event* is a situation that is perceived by the person experiencing it as violating an important moral value in a high-stakes context. These violations may be:

- Something you have done, or failed to do

- Something that someone else has done, or failed to do, to you or for you

- Something you have witnessed

- Something you learned about after it had already happened

These experiences often create strong moral emotions and judgments, arising in the moment of the event or afterward. *Healing from the suffering that emerges from struggling against this kind of pain is the focus of this workbook.*

What Makes an Event Morally Injurious?

As just noted, morally injurious events violate your deeply held values, and the stakes for these events are high. Let's take a closer look at these two characteristics.

Deeply Held Values

First, these events include *actions (or inactions) that violate your moral values.* As we will discuss in chapter 3, *moral values* are those guiding principles that help us establish or maintain connections and cohesion so we can survive and thrive in our relationships and communities. Common moral values include caring, kindness, belonging, being loving, and providing safety; there are many others. Living in line with our moral values gives life meaning, purpose, and fulfillment, not only for ourselves but also for our communities.

When your moral values are violated, this is potentially a morally injurious event. We say "potentially" morally injurious because different individuals as well as different communities have varying values or may prioritize values differently. An event that is morally injurious to one person may not be so for another. But certainly when we make choices or witness choices made by others that are contrary to our moral values, we may experience deep pain. We may feel less a part of our communities. We may become disconnected from what gives us purpose or meaning in life.

High-Stakes Context

Incidents in which our values are violated can be more or less severe, with a range of different consequences. For an incident to rise to the level of a morally injurious event, it must *happen in a high-stakes context where serious physical or psychological harm is likely.*

Robert's experience is an example of an event that meets these two criteria. Robert perceived that his actions (responding to a text while driving with his kids in the car) and his inactions (not ensuring that they put on their seat belts) violated his deeply held values of caring for and protecting his family. Although he did not realize how high the stakes were in advance of the event, the outcome—the death of his child—revealed the terrible significance of his choices.

Violating Values

Values serve as our guiding lights as we travel the path of life, showing us the way, illuminating what is important to us. When we live in line with our values, life feels more vital, purposeful, and fulfilling. For instance, if being caring toward others is your personal value, then behaving in ways that are caring will feel meaningful. When we act in ways that do not align with our values, we may find that life seems a bit less meaningful, colorful, or complete. For example, if you value kindness yet find yourself treating others in unkind ways, you may feel guilty and sad—and probably upset with yourself.

There are many ways in which we can violate our values. These could be pure mistakes—a temporary lapse in judgment, an accident, or an oversight. These incidents can be uncomfortable, but we tend to learn from them, perhaps make amends, and move on. But sometimes values violations have more significant consequences, such as losing a friend, a job, or a marriage. These types of violations might include conscious acts such as lying, stealing, or cheating, which often lead to greater moral pain. We'll talk more about these sorts of events later in this chapter.

So, what makes a values violation potentially morally injurious? It depends on what's at stake during the event.

What's at Stake?

Context—that is, the situation surrounding the values violation—is part of what elevates it to a morally injurious event. The stakes must be high. There is an elevated risk of actual physical or psychological harm—a real probability of injury or death. Indeed, you can see the importance of the stakes when you look at where the concept of moral injury was first introduced—in the aftermath of war.

Clinicians caring for military personnel returning from combat noticed that some veterans were most affected by guilt and anger about the choices they had made in combat—choices that led to harm or death for others or that involved behavior, such as war crimes, that was inconsistent with their values. Think about the stakes involved in combat, and you can see both the horrors that happen and the values that might be at risk. This is only one example, however. Morally injurious events can occur in many different contexts, for example:

- Harm to the innocent through action or inaction

- Extreme or unjustified violence

- Apparent failure to do the "right" thing when someone is or has been hurt or killed

- Tragic mistakes or oversights

- Perceived betrayal (especially by trusted others)

In most communities worldwide, these kinds of events violate important socially recognized values, leading to costly outcomes. These events are potentially morally injurious not only for the person responsible for the harm, but also for the victims, witnesses, or other survivors.

Passage of Time and the Morally Injurious Event

As Robert responds to the painful consequences of his car wreck, he is likely to feel immediate mental and emotional pain. However, painful reactions to morally injurious events can occur even years after they happen. In some morally injurious situations, the actions we take at the moment may seem to make sense. But later, painful thoughts and emotions may surface as we recognize the moral violation.

Consider the earlier example: a service member kills a child in combat because the child was wearing a vest that appeared to be an explosive device. If later the soldier learns that the child was only wearing a padded coat, the service member may experience deep pain at having taken an innocent life. In other cases, people may begin to struggle long after the event. This is more likely to happen if someone moves from one community, with its own set of moral values (like the military), to another community with a different set of values (like civilian communities). They may suddenly see that their actions that were aligned with the first group's values may be misaligned with the second group's values. We'll talk about this last situation more in chapter 3.

Awareness and the Morally Injurious Event

Robert, frustrated and tired, wasn't operating at his best. As he forgot to double check his son's seat belt, then impulsively looked at a text while driving, it's clear he'd lost awareness of the possible consequences. This was a values violation based on making a decision (really, failing to stop and think before making a decision) without awareness of the likely outcome. In other cases, a person *is* aware of the action and its consequences at the time of the violation but chooses to do it anyway. In either event, if the stakes are high, the event may be considered morally injurious.

In the following exercise, we invite you to reflect on your own experiences. You can start to better understand your moral pain by identifying when and where it started. Because these experiences are deeply personal and painful, we strongly encourage you to first find a quiet place where you feel safe. Make sure that you can stay with this exercise for ten to twenty minutes. If you think you might need support, make sure someone who can provide it is nearby.

Exercise 1.1: Noticing the Beginning: Your Personal Experience

When you're ready, answer the following questions:

1. How old were you when your morally injurious event occurred (if you have had more than one, include each age):

    _____

2. When did you first notice the mental and emotional pain of the event? If it didn't show up right away, how much time passed before you began to experience this pain?

    _____

    _____

3. Who was with you at the time? Who were the important people in your life at that time? Did they know about the event?

    _____

    _____

4. Briefly name or describe this event or events. Just a few words will do. The goal is only to clearly identify the event(s) that caused the pain that led you to pick up this book.

    _____

    _____

    _____

    _____

Take a few moments after answering these questions to reflect on what you have written. Notice whether it has been a long time since the event or the event was more recent. Notice the depth of your struggle with the pain of this experience. You don't need to do anything with what you are feeling or thinking right now. Just be *aware* of your experience.

We will continue to help you understand and work on the injury as we move through the book. In that effort, let's continue to learn more about morally injurious events and explore a few more examples.

Other Dimensions of Morally Injurious Events

To understand the different ways in which a person—a victim, the person responsible, or a witness—can experience a morally injurious event, it helps to consider how these events line up along two different dimensions. The first dimension answers this question: Whose behavior led to the violation? This person may be you, someone else, or a group, institution, or organization.

The second dimension answers this question: Did someone *do* something *wrong* or did someone *fail* to do something *right*? That is, was it an act of *commission* (something you or someone else *did*) or an act of *omission* (something you or someone else *failed to do*)? These dimensions are illustrated in the four-quadrant diagram.

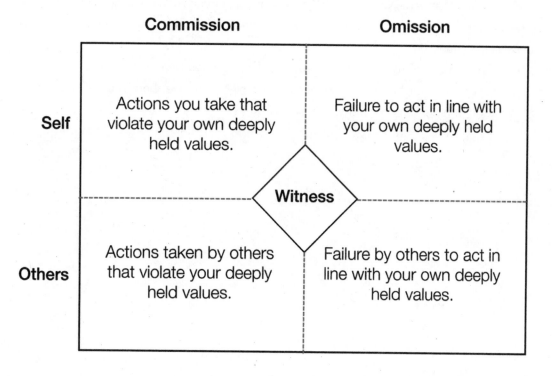

Dimensions of Moral Violations

Note: Morally injurious events often do not fall into only one of the four quadrants. The dotted lines in the diagram represent how one event may cut across two, three, or even all four quadrants. Additionally, a violation may cause injury to someone who is neither the responsible party nor the victim. The box in the center of the diagram represents the position of the witness: walled off behind the solid lines, unable to influence the violation but left to experience the painful outcomes nonetheless.

Learning about these aspects of morally injurious events and identifying which kind they experienced often helps people to better understand their responses. Before you decide where your moral injury fits, take another look at the diagram, then read the following stories of other people who went through a violation of their values.

Exercise 1.2: Stories of Violated Values

In this exercise, you'll meet three people who experienced values violations that could lead to moral injury. These are ordinary people who found themselves in situations where the stakes were high and the choices made had significant moral consequences. As you read each story, notice the moral values that were likely violated. Was it an act of commission or omission? Did someone in the story violate their own values or those of someone else? There may be more than one answer to each question.

Also take a moment to consider how you might react if you were one of the people in the story. What emotions might show up? What thoughts might you have about yourself or others?

We begin with the story of Henry.

• Henry's Story

Henry was a Marine Corps corporal assigned as the leader of a team ordered to do a house-to-house search for an insurgent. Henry's team forcefully entered the home of the target. It was a chaotic scene, with the marines shouting and the family screaming. When they found the target—the father of the family—they moved aggressively toward him. One of Henry's men struck the man in the abdomen with the butt of his weapon. The marines subdued the man while Henry zip-tied his hands together and stood him up to take him away.

When the marine hit the man in the stomach, Henry had a gut reaction that something was wrong. Then Henry saw the family's youngest child, a girl of about five—the same age as his own daughter. He had a sudden image of his daughter, watching horrified as he was struck, subdued, and tied up. He felt overcome with the wrongness of what was happening. Over time, the images of that incident wouldn't subside, and guilt and shame about what had happened began to haunt him, having a significant impact on the way he lived his life.

What moral value(s) may have been violated in this story? Whose values were they?

_____

_____

_____

_____

In what quadrant(s) of the diagram do you think Henry might experience the violation?

_____

What thoughts and emotions might you have had if you were Henry?

_____

_____

_____

• Mae's Story

One night, Mae, a volunteer firefighter, responded to an apartment fire. When Mae's crew arrived, large portions of an apartment building were engulfed in flames. Mae learned there was a child trapped in one of the apartments on the third floor. When she entered the third-floor hallway, Mae heard cries coming from the apartment. The fire had worked its way through the ceiling, and the unit was filling with smoke. As she entered, Mae could see the child on the floor on the other side of the room, reaching her hand toward Mae. Mae called to the girl, but the girl was too scared to move. Suddenly, the ceiling gave way, making it much more challenging to reach the girl. The fire grew more intense between them. The girl screamed, but Mae could not bring herself to pass through the flames. Fearing for her own life, Mae exited the apartment. The girl did not survive.

What moral value(s) may have been violated in this story? Whose values were they?

_____

_____

_____

_____

In what quadrant(s) of the diagram do you think Mae might experience the violation?

_____

What thoughts or emotions might you have had if you were Mae?

_____

_____

_____

• *Ellen's Story*

Ellen is a college freshman. During her first semester, Ellen attended a party where she met two men who lived in the dorm next to her. That night, the two men followed Ellen back to her dorm, where they raped her. The next day, Ellen told her story to a school counselor. The counselor asked Ellen whether she'd been drinking alcohol at the party. When Ellen reported that she had not, the counselor asked, "Then why did you let them follow you back to your room?" Overcome with anger, disappointment, and shame, Ellen quickly left the counselor's office. For the rest of the school year, Ellen struggled to keep up her grades. She withdrew from the friends she'd begun making. Over the summer, when Ellen returned home, her parents chastised her for her poor grades. She had not yet told them about the rape. Hoping they would understand and support her, Ellen finally shared her story with her parents. However, they shamed her and scolded her for "partying instead of studying." Rather than return to college, Ellen took a job at a local restaurant. She moved into a small apartment with three of her coworkers and began to rely on marijuana to cope with her intense, painful thoughts and feelings about herself, her assailants, and her family.

What moral value(s) may have been violated in this story? Whose values were they?

_____

_____

_____

_____

In what quadrant(s) of the diagram do you think Ellen might experience the violation?

_____

What thoughts or emotions might you have had if you were Ellen?

_____

_____

_____

These stories reflect violations of moral values as well as high-stakes situations—threats to life as well as to physical and psychological integrity. They can be called morally injurious events, just like the story of Robert. They also include different dimensions of behavior.

Henry participated in *and* observed others taking actions that violated his values of integrity and of caring for children. He experienced acts of commission by self and others. Mae found herself in a tragic situation. She acted in a way inconsistent with her value of providing safety for others. In an act of omission, she failed to save the child. Ellen experienced an act of commission by others (the men who raped her) as well as acts of omission by the counselor and her parents, who invalidated her pain, betrayed her trust, and insulted her integrity.

The Pain and Suffering of Other Types of Values Violations

In these three stories, the values violations and high-stakes situations are relatively clear. There are other situations in which moral violations may occur, yet the stakes are not quite as high, or the situation is challenging in different ways. In determining whether *moral injury* is the outcome, the high stakes of the event are an important marker.

Because this book is for everyone struggling with moral pain and seeking to reengage their values and improve their lives, let's look at examples of moral violations that may not be considered morally injurious within the context of this book, but may still lead to painful thoughts, feelings, and behaviors.

Let's consider an extramarital affair. Participating in an affair can undoubtedly be a moral violation if the people involved hold the values of integrity and faithfulness. The person in the relationship who remained faithful can feel betrayal, disgust, mistrust, and anger. The person who had the affair could also feel moral pain in the form of guilt, shame, and self-condemnation. Indeed, the outcome may be quite devastating. Even though, as we are defining it here, it doesn't rise to the level of moral injury, an affair can absolutely lead to moral pain and suffering. This being the case, those suffering from moral pain of this nature may also benefit from working through this book.

Other examples of behaviors that may violate values and potentially lead to moral pain include:

- Engaging in long-term substance abuse, leading to adverse effects on family and friends

- Stealing from family members or others to support an addiction like gambling

- Turning your back on a friend in need

- Causing destruction to property or relationships (where injury or death doesn't occur)

- Lying or cheating in ways that damage relationships or violate community norms

There are many ways that a values violation can lead to suffering and pain. Whether your experience of a painful values violation happened in high-stakes circumstances or not, you can benefit from the process of moral healing. You may still be unsure whether your experience is a moral injury as we have defined it here. It may comfort you to know that researchers are still working to more fully define morally injurious events and moral injury. We do know that people can struggle from different levels and types of moral violations. And all are welcome to discover the path of healing through the work in this book.

Your Story: Exploring Your Own Experience with Violated Values

Now that you've learned more about the dimensions of morally injurious events and read several stories of people who experienced violations of their most deeply held values, take some time to think about the experience(s) you identified.

Exercise 1.3: Your Experience

Thinking about the moral violation(s) you are working on, go back to the Dimensions of Moral Violations diagram and place a check mark in the quadrant(s) that most closely match your experience. The next step is a writing exercise. Because this work is deeply personal and can be quite painful, we encourage you to find a quiet place where you feel safe and can spend fifteen to thirty minutes on reflection and writing. Seek out support if you need it.

In the space provided, reflect on your experience of your moral injury. You can make a few notes or, if you like, make a drawing to represent the event. If you need more space to write, use additional sheets of paper or a tablet or computer. However you approach this exercise, take care. You're not trying to relive the event; rather, you're approaching the memory of the event with openness and curiosity. We hope you will learn something about the event that you may not have noticed before—something that lays the foundation for the exercises you will complete in later chapters.

Note: If you are worried that others may access this book and you do not want them to see what you have written, we suggest you write only about some of the thoughts or emotions you experienced about the event. We want you to feel safe in exploring your moral injury.

_____

_____

_____

_____

_____

_____

_____

_____

When you are finished writing, spend some time reflecting on what you've written, and then answer the following questions:

1. In what context did this event occur? Where did it happen? When? Who was present? What happened before? What happened after?

    _____

    _____

    _____

    _____

    _____

2. Whose actions or inactions led to the violation?

    _____

    _____

    _____

3. What important moral value was violated? (We'll talk more about moral values in future chapters. It's okay if you don't have this answer just yet; simply consider your values and make some notes.)

    _____

    _____

    _____

4. What were your reactions to that event? Notice particularly strong emotions and thoughts that emerged, and what your actions were in that moment.

    _____

    _____

    _____

5. How does this experience continue to affect you today?

_____

_____

_____

_____

_____

When you are finished writing and answering the questions, notice the important work you've just done. Take a moment to appreciate the healing journey you have begun.

As you read this book and complete the exercises, you will revisit the writing you just completed. Your story may change over time, and you may find that different aspects of your story stand out more or less. You may discover other parts of your memories that have been hidden or buried for a while. Be curious, notice your experience, and know that your emotions and thoughts about the event will likely keep evolving. This is part of the process. Hang in there—learning to live your values is worth the journey.

Summary

In this chapter, we introduced the concept of morally injurious events, and you began to explore how they might happen. Most important, you started the work of uncovering and exploring your own experiences with values violations that can lead to moral pain and even moral injury. You will have many opportunities to revisit and even add to your story as you embark on the healing process.

In closing this chapter, we want to again acknowledge a truth about nearly all morally injurious events: they are deeply, often unspeakably painful. The self-blame, shame, and regret; the anger and disgust; and even hatred—all are immensely challenging and can lead to suffering. For some of you reading this book, the pain and suffering of a morally injurious event has been haunting you for years, even changing the way you live in the world. Its impact on you has likely been deep and wide. You may have despaired of ever finding a path to healing. We recognize that the work of healing will take time as well as personal reflection and action. However, your first efforts have begun.

Now that we have explored some of the qualities of morally injurious events, we will help you distinguish between moral pain and moral suffering, as well as how and why we may begin to suffer after a morally injurious event. In this next chapter, we will see how moral pain itself is not the problem. What really creates suffering are the costly and unworkable attempts to undo, turn off, or rid yourself of that pain. Those efforts threaten your wholeness and connectedness, preventing you from following your moral compass. They lead to the lived suffering of moral injury.

CHAPTER 2

When Pain Becomes Suffering

We cannot always control everything that happens to us in life, but we can control how we respond.

—L. Lionel Kendrick

Pain is a universal experience. In chapter 1, we began the process of understanding different kinds of morally injurious events that can lead to moral pain. In this chapter, we will look more closely at how we respond to emotional and psychological pain. Of course, pain is unpleasant, and most of us would prefer to avoid it. Yet pain serves a purpose. It is an important signal. It alerts us to something that requires prompt attention and perhaps action.

So we ask you: Once you understand your pain's purpose, what will your relationship with your pain be? Will you struggle *against* your pain and then begin to suffer? Or will you turn *toward* the pain, face its urgency, and meet it, to learn from it and direct your energy toward living a vital life?

Answering these questions requires a bit of work and discovery. In this chapter, we will explore the difference between pain and suffering. This will be a guide, helping you consider your relationship with moral pain.

The Purpose of Pain

Recall a time when you sliced your finger in the kitchen or suffered another accidental injury. How much this hurts depends on how deeply you were cut, but even the most superficial nick will signal you to respond. The milder pain of a small cut alerted you to apply some direct pressure to stop the bleeding, then to gently wash the cut, protect it with a bandage or liquid sealant, and carry on. The more intense pain of a deeper cut may have signaled you to get help, such as going to a clinic or, if truly warranted, the ER to get stitches. Whether the injury was large or small, what thoughts crossed your mind? What was your emotional response? Write these here:

_____

_____

_____

Maybe you thought something like *I should be more careful* or *I need to remember that this knife is especially sharp.* By triggering thoughts like these, pain teaches us to avoid the *source* of that pain in the future.

Now, you might also be thinking, *Yes, but physical pain is different from mental and emotional pain.* In some ways this is true. However, the core purpose of physical pain and that of mental or emotional pain may be less different than you think. Learning more about the mental and emotional aspects of *moral pain* will help you do the work in this book.

Just as physical pain is intended to alert you that something may be wrong with your body, moral pain alerts you that something may have violated your moral values. Even further, moral pain alerts you to moral violation in your relationships or your social world. Many of the emotions experienced inside of moral pain serve social purposes. The painful emotion of shame tells you that one of your values (such as honor) has been threatened. Shame brings an urge to withdraw so others in your community won't see your shame and vulnerability. If you follow this urge, you may feel isolated and lonely. When people struggle to hide or deny their moral pain in this way, they tend to suffer both personally and socially.

We will explore the social nature of moral values more fully in chapter 3. For now, we will explore how our moral pain can motivate us to pay attention to our social world, taking steps to protect ourselves and our relationships in our community. Let's start by looking at two forms of moral pain—*moral emotions* and *moral judgments*.

Moral Pain: Moral Emotions

Like pain, emotion is a universal human experience. And much like physical pain, emotions send important internal signals. Emotions prompt us to act. They can motivate us to respond, and they can drive us to behave in certain ways, depending on the situation. Moral emotions prompt action, too. They motivate important social behavior.

Humans aren't just wired to experience and express our own emotions; we are also wired to be aware of and respond to the emotions of those around us. Emotional expressions such as laughing, smiling, or tearful eyes send social signals. While we experience emotions internally, we also express them outwardly. Let's look specifically at moral emotions.

Moral Emotions Are Social Emotions

Moral emotions are those emotions most closely connected to social relationships. They include empathy, pride, contempt, and anger, to name just a few. Moral emotions—those that align with the *morality of the heart,* as discussed in the introduction—make us aware of what is going on in our social environment. They prompt us to take actions that will be beneficial to our social group. The more painful moral emotions arise when the actions or inactions of ourselves or others violate important social (moral) values. These moral emotions signal a moral violation or a potentially morally injurious event.

Some painful moral emotions, such as embarrassment, guilt, and shame, are *self-directed.* They arise when you have engaged in actions that threaten your social bonds—that is, when you have participated in violations of shared moral values. In many situations, these emotions prompt us to act to reconcile with others. They inspire us to repair relationships and realign with our moral value(s). But they can also prompt us to withdraw from conflict or from friends and family.

There are also more pleasant or satisfying self-directed moral emotions, such as pride. Whereas guilt is like a red light, signaling you to stop the morally transgressive behavior (and/or to not repeat that behavior in the future), pride is more like a green light, prompting you to proceed with the action.

Unpleasant *other-directed* moral emotions such as anger, contempt, or disgust arise when we are offended by the behaviors of others. That is, other-directed emotions arise when we think their behavior presents a threat to our own well-being or our community or group. These emotions may motivate us to express disapproval, which motivates others to work on repairing relationships, realigning with values, and restoring the community. There are also pleasant other-directed moral emotions, such as awe and gratitude, that arise when others' actions support community values and social relationships.

Table 2.1 presents moral emotions that commonly follow morally injurious events, some of the cause(s) of these emotions, and some of the behaviors they tend to motivate. Two are listed as self-directed and four as other-directed, but any of the six can be experienced as self- or other-directed.

Table 2.1: Moral Emotions: Causes and Outcomes

	Moral Emotion	What Causes It	What Behaviors It Motivates
Self-directed	Guilt	Evaluation of one's actions as wrong or a failure to do the right thing	Action to repair the transgression; decision not to repeat the behavior; withdrawal
	Shame	Negative evaluation of one's core self (like *I'm a bad parent* or *I'm a monster*)	Withdrawal, isolation, disconnection from others
Other-directed	Anger	Perception that someone or something else violated one's morals, values, or expectations	Pursuit of resolution or recompense, possibly through aggression; withdrawal from the relationship
	Contempt	Determination that someone is not worthy of respect or approval	Corrective instruction of the offender(s); distancing from the contemptible persons or behaviors
	Disgust	Perceived violation or desecration of something important, valuable, or sacred	Preservation of personal wellness by withdrawal; aggression toward perceived repugnant persons or behaviors
	Hatred	Extreme dislike, usually developed over time; often connected to anger, contempt, and disgust	Distancing from hated other(s) through avoidance and/or aggression intending to push other(s) away

Each of us has a personal filter that may change the way we experience the moral emotions listed in the table. Our purpose here is to highlight how these emotions *can* function—in other words, how they might be able to serve (rather than hinder) you and others.

Exercise 2.1: Identifying Moral Emotions

1. Take some time to reflect on what you felt at the time of your moral violation written about in chapter 1.

2. Identify the moral emotions that you may have felt or continue to feel in response to this morally injurious event.

3. Read through the "Moral Emotion" column in the table with your event in mind. On the table, circle or highlight the emotions that seem to be part of your experience.

4. Reflect for a moment on each circled emotion. Do you experience them as self- or other-directed? Pay attention to where in your body you experienced or continue to experience these emotions.

5. Take a few moments to write about your observations:

   _____

   _____

   _____

   _____

   _____

6. Recall what was going on inside you at the time of the morally injurious event. Noticing the emotions you just identified, how did you respond when you experienced those emotions? What actions did you take when they arose?

   _____

   _____

   _____

7. It may have taken some time—even years—for you to become fully aware of these moral emotions. How did you respond, then or now, to these moral emotions? What thoughts did you experience along with these emotions?

_____

_____

_____

8. How do these emotional experiences affect you today?

_____

_____

_____

As you complete this exercise, know that it's normal to find it difficult or emotionally charged to reflect on your experience. This is precisely why we call it a moral injury. You haven't had the chance to heal from this wound, so if it feels tender, have patience. Sometimes these types of injuries have been a part of someone's life for a long time. Healing requires time, patience, and persistence. Indeed, there is more work to do. And we need to explore both your emotional reactions to the experience and your thinking about it.

Moral Pain: Moral Judgments

Thoughts that are a part of our moral life are called *moral judgments*. These thoughts are often intimately linked to moral pain. They are our evaluations of our actions or the actions of others related to the moral violation. These judgments align with the *morality of the mind* that we discussed in the introduction, and they're often negative. They can persist for a very long time. And importantly, they are not quickly or easily forgotten.

Sometimes we direct moral judgments at ourselves. These might include thoughts such as *I did something bad*, or *How could I fail in such a horrible way?* Sometimes we direct moral judgments at others, like *They did something bad* or *How could they do such a thing?*

Although these thoughts may be uncomfortable, they still provide valuable information. For instance, if you have a thought that you did something bad or that someone should not have behaved in a particular way, you become aware that something was out of line with your values.

Consider the following questions with respect to your experience of moral injury:

1. What moral values were violated?

2. What are some ways you could repair the damage done?

3. What future behaviors would be more aligned with your values?

Your answers can give you a sense of how your moral judgments provide crucial information about the values violation *and* how you might repair the damage.

You may already be asking about what it means to repair what happened. We will get there, but we don't want to move too fast and miss important parts of the healing. Hang in there as we continue to discover more about moral emotions and moral judgments.

Exercise 2.2: Identifying Moral Judgments

Review Table 2.1, Moral Emotions: Causes and Outcomes. Keeping your morally injurious event(s) in mind, read each of the three columns, noticing the emotion, the causes, and the behavior it tends to motivate. See if you can discover what judgments and thoughts tend to be triggered for you when you consider each of the categories. Take a few moments to reflect on these judgments, not letting yourself get too caught up in them. Write about your experience by answering the following questions:

1. Become aware of what was going on at the time of your morally injurious event. What kinds of judgments or thoughts did you have at that time? Do these same judgments continue to trouble you today?

   _____

   _____

   _____

   _____

   _____

2. It may have also been some time, years even, before these moral judgments came into your awareness. If so, when did you notice them? What was going on at that time?

_____

_____

_____

3. How did you respond to these moral judgments, or how do you respond today? How do these judgments define you or affect you now?

_____

_____

_____

4. Do you hold any broad, general moral judgments about other individuals, groups, or a higher power, related to your moral injury? What are these judgments? How do they define or affect you today?

_____

_____

_____

In considering these judgments, see if you can be curious but not harsh with yourself. We will work to change your relationship with these thoughts, but we also want to notice if they have any purpose. Do they tell you something about your values?

Mind and Heart: Working Together

Our struggle with moral pain can get complicated when morality of the mind and heart aren't working together. When they *are* working together, guilt may appear about a morally injurious event alongside the thought, *I should have saved them,* or contempt may show up with the thought, *He should never have treated me that way.* In these cases, the morality of your mind and the morality of your heart are working together, interpreting the violation in the same way. Motivated by those thoughts and emotions, you may then engage in behaviors to repair or make amends for the violation. In this case, pain—though uncomfortable—is a useful signal, a teacher who, when we listen, guides us toward healing.

Even when mind and heart are aligned, though, healing isn't easy, nor is it always the outcome. In response to morally injurious experiences, some people withdraw or hide. They might punish themselves or believe they deserve to be alone. They let their thoughts and emotions take over—pushing them *even further* away from acting on their values. This is *suffering*, often more excruciating than emotional pain.

Mind and Heart: Working Apart

For an example of when minds and hearts don't work hand in hand, let's return to the story of Henry in the last chapter. He logically acknowledged (with the morality of the mind) that his team had completed their assigned mission. They had followed the rules of engagement. At the same time, he also experienced emotions of guilt (morality of the heart) for his role in taking a father from his family (self-directed) and of contempt for the institution and the leaders who assigned him such a mission (other-directed).

Moral injury can be complex and demanding, a voyage through turbulent waters. It can be a challenge to find a way to hold both the morality of heart and the morality of the mind so you can stay at the helm of the ship and sail forward, but it is important to healing. In choosing to steer the ship, you can use the information provided by your thoughts and feelings to reengage with moral values. If you leave the helm and simply get tossed about in the waves, then you are lost to the judgments of the mind and the pain of the heart. They take over, and you end up behaving in ways that are even more out of line with your values, hiding in the hull, trying to make the turbulence stop. The result is even more suffering.

The Costs of Choosing Suffering

The suffering that results from struggling against moral pain can show up in many ways. For instance, sometimes moral judgments grow to represent the totality of a person or a group of people, rather than just the behavior that happened at the time of the event. Such self-directed moral judgments might include *I am a bad person* or *I am unforgivable, irredeemable* or *I am a monster who only hurts the people around me.* Other-directed moral judgments might include *Men like that are a waste of space* or *No one in authority can be trusted to have their subordinates' best interests in mind.* For people with or without religious or spiritual beliefs, these types of global moral judgments may be directed at God or religions—*All religions are evil,* for example. Some people may have the thought that God has abandoned them, or they may conclude that God does not exist if such moral violations can be allowed to happen. The painful judgments continue, and the response to them can create suffering.

In exploring both moral emotions and moral judgments related to your morally injurious event, you may now better understand how to label and describe your experience. You may also notice which behaviors they tend to motivate and how these experiences influence your life. Even with this new knowledge, we want you to recognize that simply being more aware of your experiences won't be enough to enable moral healing.

Exploring these experiences can further the process of organizing the story of your morally injurious event(s)—a helpful undertaking. Identifying your experiences related to the morally injurious event sets your feet on the path to healing. However, a significant challenge remains. You may ask, "What next?" Other questions might include, "Now that I have clarified and labeled my experiences and I have noted how they have impacted me, how do I get rid of these experiences?" or "How do I overcome these thoughts and feelings so that I can have my life back?" or "How do I get these experiences under control?"

There are no easy answers to these questions. But not for the reasons you may think. From a certain perspective, these questions cannot be answered. Not because you or we aren't smart enough, but because changing your relationship with your emotions and thoughts simply doesn't work that way. Indeed, trying not to feel and think often leads to more of the same.

The Promise and Perils of the Human Mind

The human mind is amazing. Its development and growth over time have expanded our capacity to create, communicate, and discover. Using our minds, we have built cities, traveled to the moon, developed ways to kill viruses and bacteria, and learned to survive and thrive in ways that no other animal on earth has done. We have become the dominant species on the planet. Our ability to learn and expand our wealth of knowledge has all been done with the mind. Incredible!

Yet even though our minds have been a blessing—enabling us to be intimate, to plan, and to problem solve—they have also been a burden. We don't use our minds only to create what can be good; we can also use them in ways that are not so helpful. For instance, we can dwell for extended periods on long-ago events. We can follow rules without any kind of flexibility, leading us to be rigid in our behavior. We can imagine future terrors—even our own death—and respond as if they are happening now, becoming afraid of something that hasn't yet happened.

For all the wonderful things our minds can do, there are plenty of things that are unpleasant, even hurtful (like calling ourselves names and criticizing ourselves or others). One important thing that minds do, which is particularly relevant to the issue at hand, is to try to control. Minds try to solve what can't be solved. They try to "solve" the past or emotions. They try to "solve" judgments and thoughts that we don't like. It is no accident that we've learned to do this; our minds are designed to protect us by finding and labeling perceived problems—including unwanted emotions, thoughts, and memories—and getting them under control.

Minds try to control through problem solving, and minds are very good at solving problems most of the time. It might take extra effort and energy if it is a particularly tricky problem, but persistence often pays off. Indeed, this works very well in the world around us. If you have a broken chair, get some glue or a hammer and nails. If you have scrapes and dents in the wall, get some filler and paint. If you have dirty or damaged carpet, clean it or pull it up, throw it out, and replace it. In the world outside of our physical body, in our environment, if something is broken, we can fix it. We figure it out and go.

But what about the world within us? What if your mind is telling you that *you* are broken, that you have scrapes and dents, that you are dirty or damaged? Well, if your mind is like most minds, it says, *Figure out how to fix it, and fix it.* Yet day after day, strategy after strategy, "fixing" your thoughts and emotions doesn't work. The effort never seems to pay off. The emotions and thoughts return again and again. Indeed, for some, the problem intensifies. Now you have your pain *plus* your longstanding and costly efforts to control the pain. This is *suffering*.

The Paradox of Trying to "Fix" Moral Pain: A Road to Suffering

Control works when you have a cut on your skin. You find a bandage or get stitches. The pain makes it undeniable that this should be done. You control your behavior and your environment to help yourself heal. However, when we engage this same strategy to try to fix emotional pain and judgments, something different happens. The very attempts to control that worked in the world outside us fail in the world within us. A paradox unfolds.

Control of what goes on within us seems to make the problem worse. Indeed, the more you try not to feel, the more afraid of your emotions you become. The more you try not to judge, the more you may encounter the judgmental thoughts. Trying to control the emotions and thoughts occurring inside you leads to more of the same. Let's test this out.

Exercise 2.3: The Paradox of Emotion and Thought Control

Reflect on your completion of Exercises 2.1 and 2.2. Become aware again of the feelings and thoughts associated with your moral injury. Now answer the following questions:

1. How long have you had your moral pain? _____ years _____ months _____ days

2. Knowing how long this pain has been with you, explore, as best you can remember, every way you have tried to fix it, overcome it, get rid of it, forget about it, and so on. List each effort, both "good" strategies (like coping skills, work) and "bad" strategies (like substance use, ignoring, hiding):

_____   _____

_____   _____

_____   _____

_____   _____

_____   _____

_____   _____

_____   _____

_____   _____

3. Now notice how hard you have tried. Notice how much effort you have put into "fixing the problem." Did it work? Did it get you where you want to be? Reflect by writing here:

_____

_____

_____

If you discovered that each of your efforts to control the thoughts and emotions related to your moral injury didn't pay off in the way that you would have hoped or wanted, we are not surprised, and you are not alone. What if the constant struggle to control your emotions and thoughts actually is the problem? We agree that you can influence and maybe even control your thoughts and feelings *some* of the time. We have all had the experience of moving past something or directing our attention to something else, then forgetting about what was bothering us. But the biggies, the really painful stuff—those don't just quietly go away.

Even with excellent plans and sincere elbow grease, we cannot clean and simply throw out what *seems* to be the dirty and damaged stuff inside us—even if our mind tells us we can. Problem solving applied to emotions and thoughts backfires. It works well in the outside world, but it falls terribly short of its promise when it comes to the world within us.

It's worth noting that this failure to control your thoughts and feelings is not your fault. We have all learned that we *should* be able to do this. We have all been told that we should be able to "get over it," "move on," or "let it go." We live in a social system that has given us false hope about the power of problem solving applied to the very natural human response of emotional pain.

Our Invitation to You

Before going any further, consider this statement: moral pain is not a problem, not a sign of weakness, not an indicator of brokenness, not a flaw or a fault. Experiencing moral pain is a sign that you are whole and you are human. Your moral compass is intact and fully operational. Your system for signaling violations of moral values is working, and it's giving you information that can help you move forward in a way that aligns with your values and may allow you to connect with others—even though you or they have been harmed in the past.

Moral pain is, simply put, painful. It is unpleasant, so it's natural to wish to get rid of it. However, moral pain is part of that system of morality that has helped humans to flourish and build social communities. Moral pain, like physical pain, *is* signaling us to avoid something, to fix something, to control something. However, also like physical pain, moral pain is telling us to focus on the *source* of the pain, not only the pain itself. To that end, we will advocate acceptance of moral pain *in the service of vital, vibrant, meaningful living.* As you consider acceptance and willingness to embrace pain, you may notice anxiety, fear, or doubt showing up within you. With those emotions present, journey forward with us.

Willingness: The Alternative to Control

People and their emotions are like sunsets; they are not like math problems (adapted from Wilson & DuFrene, 2008). Emotions are here to be experienced, not solved. If there is no way to "fix" or eliminate your moral pain, then what do you do? There is an alternative to problem solving: willingness. *Willingness, or acceptance, is the avenue to healing.*

At this moment, you may have doubts; perhaps you have tried a version of acceptance before. But we ask for your patience yet again. The willingness to experience is a muscle you'll need to build up, a process to be continually engaged in. It involves openness and choice. Willingness is a path back to living your values, even—perhaps especially—those values that have been violated.

Willingness is an active, conscious process. It entails releasing yourself into full acceptance while being present to the ongoing flow of internal experience and then choosing the values-based action you want to engage in. Acceptance and commitment therapy (ACT; Hayes, Strosahl, & Wilson, 2012) was developed to help those who suffer from ongoing emotional and psychological pain to return to full and meaningful lives. ACT is an evidenced-based intervention that has been used to help people overcome suffering worldwide. It uses three guiding pillars or response styles—*open, aware, engaged*—to create change. It means no longer trying to impose excessive and misapplied control but instead embracing acceptance and meaning. Through ACT, you define and explore your values and reengage with purpose and intention. ACT has helped people heal from all sorts of painful experiences; it can help you too.

ACT and Moral Healing

Using the foundations and processes of ACT, we continue on the path to healing from moral injury. The coming chapters will guide you through the main components of ACT and invite you to engage in more exercises designed to assist you in the process of healing. We will further explore when and where the mind is useful, as well as when and where it is not. We will explore openness and the power of values-based living. We will see how trying to eliminate or control pain also robs you of joy. And we will help you find ways to discover that pain is not your enemy, but is actually the very thing that makes you human.

Let's start by introducing you to ACT, as a preview for the coming chapters and the start of a solid foundation.

The Three Pillars of ACT: Open, Aware, Engaged

The processes that support openness are *willingness* and *defusion* (see box). Together they create the space and stance needed for acceptance of internal experiences. (Remember the word "stance"; we'll have more to say about it in chapter 5.) We will work to help you grow your openness and relate to your moral pain in a new way that leads to healing.

ACT Openness Processes:

- *Willingness* is a process of fostering acceptance of emotions, thoughts, and sensations while dismantling the agenda of emotional control and avoidance of pain.

- *Defusion* is the process of understanding that you have a mind and recognizing that you can "see" that you think. This understanding helps you disentangle yourself from the "mind" (fusion) *and* the kinds of thoughts and judgments that stand between you and life-enhancing activities. Defusion means simply observing the stream of your thoughts.

The processes that support awareness are *present moment* and *self-as-context* (see box). Together, they create a sense of self, experienced in the present moment, that is more than any single thought or emotion. The work undertaken in this pillar is about helping you live in the here and now—the only place where life is unfolding. It will help you view yourself as more than your pain and indeed more than any thought or emotion you might experience.

ACT Awareness Processes:

- *Present moment* is a process of helping you to show up in the present—to be here now. Living more fully present to each moment as it unfolds takes you beyond your mind and its unhelpful thoughts and connects you with a richer set of possibilities. This is the one place where you gain mindfulness of what *is* and freedom of choice.

- *Self-as-context* is a process of viewing yourself as more than simply your experiences or the individual events of your life. You are the place where internal life events (thoughts, feelings, sensations) unfold. These events rise and fall in an ongoing rhythm, and you are there for each new experience.

The processes that support engagement are *values* and *committed action* (see box). Together they create meaning and purpose in life. They are part of the reason we invite willingness as an alternative to control. In the direction of your values, by being willing to think and feel what you think and feel, you can engage life now. Values justify that stance and give life purpose.

ACT Engagement Processes:

- *Values* engagement is about focusing on giving your life a sense of meaning and direction. It allows greater flexibility than merely following social rules. Values are defined by what you *do*, not what you *think*. They are lived in the moment and guide your direction forward in life.

- *Committed action* is the process of engaging in values-aligned behavior. The ultimate goal is to build ever more expansive patterns of behavior that are consistent with your values.

Broadly speaking, ACT uses these six core processes to help people let go—not necessarily of their pain, but of their fruitless attempts to control it—to decrease suffering and create meaningful lives.

Summary

We could probably spend the remaining pages of this book describing moral violations, moral pain, and suffering. The fields of psychology, theology, philosophy, neurobiology, and evolutionary science have so much to say about these topics that we would barely skim the surface in two hundred pages. But this workbook is intended for your moral healing, so in these first two chapters we have provided a foundation from which you can begin this healing journey. As we explore the topics of ACT and healing, we'll support your healing by inviting you not only to gain new knowledge, but also to apply it by engaging in exercises. (For extra practice, read and complete the worksheet Moral Injury and the Paradox of Control downloadable at http://www.newharbinger.com/44772. See the very back of this book for more details.)

Continuing to lay the foundation of wisdom to set the context for the future work, in chapter 3 we'll explore *moral values*—those guiding principles that facilitate or maintain connection, cohesion, survival, and thriving in relationships and communities—by *mapping your moral communities*.

CHAPTER 3

Mapping Your Moral Communities

Whether we appreciate it or not, we live out our lives surrounded by an intricate pattern of social connections.... We're all embedded in this network; it affects us profoundly and we may be unaware of its existence, of its effect on us.

—Nicholas A. Christakis

When we explore morality in everyday conversations, it is often related to right and wrong. For example, a person might say, "It was wrong of you to steal my parking spot!" This kind of moral reaction comes naturally to us. In this chapter, we're going to ask you to rethink what it means for something to be "moral." We will stretch beyond the idea that morality is only about right and wrong. Although this may feel strange or unfamiliar, these new perspectives will play an essential role in your journey toward healing. After all, to know how to heal a moral injury, we must first understand how morality can be injured.

Nearly all individuals with moral injury sense a *disconnection in relationships that once were meaningful to them.* This sometimes happens because one person in the relationship caused the moral violation and it seemed to push apart those involved. Other times, such as in the story of Ellen in chapter 1, the lingering pain of a moral violation leads a person to pull away from meaningful relationships, which leaves them alone and isolated. Ellen left school and moved out of her parents' home to avoid being reminded of her rape and her perception of being blamed by her family. In this example, we can see how her response to moral pain may have led to the lived suffering of moral injury, as explained in chapter 2. Still other people with moral injury become deeply cynical about society and the value of social bonds. Although it can take different forms, social disconnection is at the core of moral injury, and reconnection plays a critical role in moral healing.

Morality Is Social

Think about this statement: Morality makes sense only in the context of social relationships. As we will explore next, looking at morality through this social lens creates new possibilities—opportunities emerge for developing and improving relationships and being involved in activities that matter to you. You'll also gain the freedom to live your values in a fuller and more fruitful way. Let's take a closer look.

The Morality of a Castaway

Perhaps at some time in your life you have read a book about a castaway stranded alone on a tropical island. Perhaps you saw the film *Cast Away* starring Tom Hanks. He plays a man stranded on an island for four years with only a volleyball that he names "Wilson." Imagine what it might be like to live a moral life in such a situation.

What are some of the most basic moral rules that many people learn growing up? Likely what comes to mind are simple rules like "Be honest," "Don't steal," and "Don't harm others." But what do these rules even mean when you're totally alone on an island? If you were marooned for an extended period, your ideas about morality might begin to lose meaning. That's not to say that you would forget what you had learned about morality. However, these teachings would no longer be useful. Morality, like other aspects of social life, generally requires that you have at least one other person to relate to for it to matter. Similarly, if you're alone on a desert island, it is hard to imagine how you might develop a moral injury, because moral violations typically involve other people. Most of us spend little or no time in such total social isolation, and doing so would be costly in terms of living a fulfilling, meaningful life.

Morality Begins at Birth

You have been in relationships all your life. At birth, you met your parents or caregivers, and perhaps others, for the first time. And suddenly the journey of negotiating the social world, including learning how to behave morally, was under way. Every person on this planet has had to face this situation—learning how to become part of a community with its own rules, values, and morality.

Likewise, your family and other groups you later became a part of did not develop this morality from scratch. They inherited and adapted rules and norms from their own communities, then passed them on to you. Whether or not you ultimately agreed with them, they instructed you not only in the logical morality of the mind but also in how to make sense of and use the morality of the heart. You learned in these relationships which values your community cared about and their degree of importance. These powerful messages likely helped to shape the choices you made and how you see yourself now as a person.

And yet, despite being so familiar, these messages do not define you. They were taught to you—you learned them from birth. Because these messages are woven into your relationship with yourself and others from such an early age, you may forget that you weren't born with them (morality of the mind). Without our noticing it, we can take these lessons for granted as absolute and unchallengeable truths, which prevents us from seeing and understanding other perspectives.

To create a more flexible way to relate to these ideas, we first need to become aware of them. So, in the following exercise, we will explore some of the different relationships you have with your morals—both the rules you have been taught and the values that those rules are connected to. Developing awareness of where your morality originated helps you understand why the violation of some values can be so incredibly painful.

Exercise 3.1: Who Were Your Moral Teachers?

Select three people from your childhood who played important roles in teaching you what to believe about how to behave. Enter their names in the boxes provided. These three may have taught you verbally (by telling you) or by example. All three may have been part of one group, or they may have come from many different times, places, and communities. As you consider these individuals, think about the moral teachings they shared with you. These lessons may be ones that were violated during your morally injurious event, or they may be ones that helped to inform the choices you made in response to it.

We understand that it is not practical for you to list all of your important teachers. The goal is not to make a complete list or to choose the most important, but to begin increasing your awareness of some of the influential people in your past or present. Understanding where your values come from is a first step to taking ownership of them—choosing which values you want to act on. Complete the exercise by writing about your personal experience with each teacher. The filled-in example can help you get started.

Example	How old were you when you learned from this person?	What was this person's role in your life?
Name: <u>Mr. Pederson</u>	<u>Fifteen</u>	<u>Volleyball coach</u>
What was the most significant moral rule they taught you?	<u>"Don't let your teammates down."</u>	
What values did this rule represent?	<u>Responsibility, commitment</u>	

Teacher #1	How old were you when you learned from this person?	What was this person's role in your life?
Name:		
What was the most significant moral rule they taught you?		
What values did this rule represent?		

Teacher #2	How old were you when you learned from this person?	What was this person's role in your life?
Name:		
What was the most significant moral rule they taught you?		
What values did this rule represent?		

Teacher #3	How old were you when you learned from this person?	What was this person's role in your life?
Name:		
What was the most significant moral rule they taught you?		
What values did this rule represent?		

When you've finished writing, consider whether you continue to think of these moral values as important in your life today. Did practicing this exercise make these values seem clearer to you? Getting clear about which moral values matter to you can help you make decisions about how to move forward in life.

Identifying some of the moral teachers in your life can help you locate the source of some of the rules you were taught about right and wrong as well as some of the values you care most about. However, you may have noticed that, even in the small sample in this exercise, you have learned different messages at different times from different people. Belonging to more than one relationship or community often means having different and sometimes conflicting moral values. This poses the potential dilemma of upholding one value while violating another.

Morality at Three Levels of Relationship

To help you disentangle the complex webs of relationships that form the contexts for morality, it helps to divide them into three levels, reflecting different types of relationships: first, your relationship with the whole community; second, your relationships with individuals within your community; and third, your relationship with yourself.

Morality and the Whole Community

You can think of a community as a group of people with shared expectations for how to cooperate. Communities have formal rules about how people should act and what things are important. They have certain group standards or goals that members are expected to support. For example, being part of a particular political party or religious organization may mean that members of that group show support for the group's ideals, such as in election campaigning or through public prayer. These behaviors signal to other members of the group that the individual is a part of the community.

By taking on roles within a community, people also begin to take on identities associated with those roles. For instance, a person's role may include being a leader, which may entail providing direction to the group or being a protector who helps preserve safety. Another person might take on the role of a healer who assists those who are suffering. These identities serve essential functions in helping individuals identify—to themselves and to others—how they fit into the community.

When getting to know someone, it's common to be asked, "What do you do?" It would be strange for you to reply, "I brush my teeth" or "I walk and talk." Although these responses might be accurate, that probably wasn't the intent of the question. More likely you would talk about what you do for employment, where you are a student, your role as a parent, or something like that.

Each of these responses helps the asker know how you fit into society. These responses also give information about which subgroups you may be a part of and which values you might feel are important. For example, if you replied that you are a teacher, the person asking might suppose that, as a teacher, you spend much of your time around children. They might assume that you prize values such as acquiring knowledge or being nurturing. In this way, social roles help simplify our interactions with one another by creating a short-hand for defining who we are in relation to others and the community as a whole.

Exercise 3.2: Discovering Your Social Roles

To help you become more aware of how your journey of healing may intersect with your social roles, read through these examples. Put a check by several roles you currently play or have played in the past. Notice if any seem particularly important to you, and add others not listed that are or have been meaningful to you.

Teacher	Follower	Comic	Peacemaker	Friend
Provider	Protector	Student	Expert	Partner
Comforter	Leader	Follower	Organizer	Volunteer
Supervisor	Coach	Employee	Citizen	Misfit

_____ _____ _____ _____ _____

Have any of these roles been affected by your moral injury? If so, consider the impact and write about it briefly:

_____

_____

_____

_____

We would not be surprised if you noticed that your social roles have been affected by your moral injury. We recognize that moral injury can influence how you experience and engage in the larger social world. This is what makes this journey of moral healing so important.

Morality and One-on-One Relationships

Communities are also made up of pairs of individuals in one-on-one relationships. Instead of asking what the group needs or what the group expects, at the one-on-one level, we ask, what does *this* person need, and what do they expect of me? These individual relationships can serve as powerful incentives for moral behavior. The emotional bond formed by living and working near others creates a sense of familiarity, safety, and loyalty that encourages us to maintain these relationships.

One-on-one relationships also provide opportunities for people to reward or punish each other's behavior. People's reactions to each other help to influence behavior, making some behavior more or less likely. If a person shares a meal with us, we might be more inclined to share a meal with them in the future. However, if a person betrays our trust, we might be more likely to shut them out of our personal lives as well as out of our social circles. Ellen's story in the first chapter illustrates the impact that feeling betrayed can have on our relationships.

Individual relationships can change, either growing or shrinking in strength and number. By repeating and expanding on these seemingly small exchanges between each other and over time, individuals create ever expanding patterns of behavior based on how they treat each other. Taken together, these kinds of one-on-one interactions between individuals are the threads within a group that help make up the fabric of the larger community. Let's take a look at some of these threads in your life.

Exercise 3.3: Discovering Your Roles in Relationships

Review the listed relationship roles and put a check by those that relate to you. Again, if there are others you would like to include, feel free to add roles in the blank spaces. As you look at each one, reflect on which relationship roles are the most meaningful to you today.

Mentor	Parent	Teammate	Trainee	Sibling
Romantic partner	Son	Friend	Daughter	Colleague
_____	_____	_____	_____	_____

Notice if these roles have been affected by your moral injury; if they have, consider the impact and write about it briefly:

_____

_____

_____

_____

_____

Again, we would not be surprised if you noticed that your relationship roles have been impacted by your moral injury. Moral injury can change how you experience and engage with people close to you.

Morality and Your Relationship with Yourself

There is a third level of relationship that is critical when it comes to morality: your relationship with yourself. We humans have the capacity for self-awareness. We can know our own emotions and thoughts and can reflect on these experiences. We can reflect on our past and imagine our future. We can also take others' perspectives and imagine what they are feeling and thinking about us. Through communication, we can express to others what we know about our thoughts and feelings. This ability—this social awareness—is incredibly useful in helping us to connect, cooperate, and grow with others.

SOCIAL AWARENESS AND YOUR RELATIONSHIP WITH YOURSELF

Social awareness has a painful side as well. When we realize that we have violated a moral value, we may feel ashamed, guilty, and embarrassed. We can picture others judging us or viewing us with contempt as a result of the violation. This capacity can become particularly destructive when we start to react to these thoughts and feelings by being harsh—or even harmful—toward ourselves.

REMEMBERING THE PAST AND YOUR RELATIONSHIP WITH YOURSELF

To understand moral injury, it is essential to zero in on your mind's ability to remember the past. This ability can sometimes be quite useful, such as when learning from past experiences to solve current problems we are facing. But the mind can also dwell endlessly on our past mistakes or hold onto grudges after we have been harmed. And when people can't forgive themselves for something they have done, they change their relationship with themselves—perhaps even leading to self-condemnation.

When your mind becomes stuck in the past, going over past events again and again, you can come to feel defined by them—trapped by events that may have long since passed. You may come to believe that an action you took in the past has tainted your very essence—so much so that you may feel that you will never be whole again. You may lose hope that you can ever move forward and create positive changes in your life or the lives of the people around you. You can begin to relate to yourself differently, perhaps harshly. When you interact with your past in this way, suffering is inevitable.

CREATING FUTURES AND YOUR RELATIONSHIP WITH YOURSELF

The mind can also be like a movie screen—a place where you can imagine a future social interaction, visualizing how that interaction might happen, even though it may never happen. We can explore these possible futures with our minds—worrying about whether they will happen and how we will respond. Unfortunately, we can get so caught up in these imagined futures that we begin to act as if they are already happening or will definitely happen. Again, you can begin to relate to yourself in a harsh way, perhaps rigidly assuming that you will ruin anything you try to build, or that others will reject you if you try to connect with them. Suffering is the inevitable outcome of relating to your future in this way.

Exercise 3.4: Discovering Your Relationship with Yourself

This exercise will help you become more aware of how your journey of healing from moral injury intersects with your relationship with yourself. Take a look at the words in the boxes and put a check by those that best describe how you tend to relate to or treat yourself, especially the ways you respond to yourself when experiencing painful moral emotions like shame or anger or when thinking about the moral injury. Again, you can add words, if needed.

Self-defeating	Nurturing	Impatient	Affirming	Neglectful
Encouraging	Self-critical	Compassionate	Doubting	Reflective
Hateful	Understanding	Misunderstanding	Forgiving	Unforgiving
Kind	Unkind	Gentle	Harsh	Fearful

_____   _____   _____   _____   _____

Notice how your relationship with yourself has been affected by moral injury. Write about this briefly:

_____

_____

_____

_____

_____

If you find suffering in your relationship with yourself, it's important to acknowledge it. Bringing awareness to how you treat yourself is relevant to how you treat others. Building a new relationship with yourself is the beginning of creating a different relationship with others, in both one-on-one relationships and communities.

Moral Healing Also Happens in Relationships

In the preceding exercises, we can see that morality occurs in the context of relationships, with others and with ourselves. This better prepares us to see how moral injury affects our ability to live full and meaningful lives. By noticing the three levels, we can begin to see how moral injury enters our networks of relationships, sending ripple effects through them. Most important, *this also means that those same relationships can become the very place where healing happens.*

As we defined it in chapter 2, moral injury is the suffering caused by unworkable or costly attempts to avoid, escape, or solve natural moral pain. If you are suffering from moral injury, you may feel the need to isolate, hide, or exclude yourself. You may reject others or push them away. Or you may feel the need to punish yourself or others. In this way, the pain caused by even a single morally injurious event can actually worsen and affect more of your life as time passes.

In your attempts to avoid moral pain, you may behave in ways that are personally harmful, such as harsh self-criticism and treating yourself as undeserving. You may find costly ways to distract from the pain, such as high-risk behaviors, substance abuse, or isolating yourself in damaging ways. But the impact doesn't stop there. The way you relate to your moral pain spreads into how you engage with other people as well. By isolating or emotionally distancing yourself, you also decrease your social connection to others around you. Sometimes avoidance strategies become so powerful that you may have difficulty fulfilling your responsibilities, thus impacting the broader community as well as your one-on-one relationships. Healing from moral injury is therefore not just about healing yourself; it is about improving your connections to others and to your communities.

Mapping Your Moral Contexts

Understanding the connections between your various groups or communities and the roles you play within them can be confusing and complicated. Often different groups or communities you are a part of have different priorities and expectations of their members. Additionally, you may notice that you play different roles in these different communities. Remember, these communities are complex; at times, they can intersect and interact with one another. To understand how your moral injury has impacted your relationships with your communities, loved ones, and yourself, you'll need to gain awareness of how these relationships, groups, and communities intersect.

To help organize these different contexts, use the worksheet in Exercise 3.5 to identify some of your most important moral contexts and some of the qualities that may differentiate them from one another. By "moral contexts" we mean the relationships between you and one or more other people. A moral context can be a relationship between you and a community of people, a handful of individuals, or even a one-on-one relationship with another person. Because your moral contexts help give meaning and significance to your experience of morality, your pursuit of moral healing will benefit from your better understanding those contexts.

Exercise 3.5: Mapping Your Moral Communities

Read and respond to the following questions and then complete the following boxes:

1. Which communities do you spend the most time in currently? For example, work, school, hobby clubs.

   _____

   _____

   _____

2. Which, if any, of the communities overlap?

   _____

   _____

   _____

3. What roles do you serve in these communities?

   _____

   _____

   _____

4. What values are most prized in these communities, for example, hard work, helping others, being a good listener?

_____

_____

_____

5. How did the morally injurious event affect your standing in these groups, if at all? Were you pushed out of a group? Did you withdraw on your own?

_____

_____

_____

6. Which communities mean the most to you?

_____

_____

_____

7. What values-consistent behaviors occur in these communities? For example, kind actions, supportive words, being dependable.

_____

_____

_____

What did you notice as you completed this exercise? What do you observe about your roles within your different groups and communities?

_____

_____

_____

_____

_____

What do you notice about your values as you express them in those groups? How has moral injury impacted the way you engage with these communities?

_____

_____

_____

_____

_____

Example Map

Group: Family

This group's priorities are...
- Togetherness
- Supporting each other
- Love

My roles in this group are...
- Provide for physical needs
- Teach good behavior
- Give discipline

Group: Marriage

This group's priorities are...
- Helping with kids
- Sharing burdens
-

My roles in this group are...
- Being a good listener
- Volunteer to help
-

You

Group: Friends

This group's priorities are...
- Relaxing
- Having fun
-

My roles in this group are...
- Be a joker
- Get people together
-

Group: Work

This group's priorities are...
- Profitability
- Efficiency
- Dependability

My roles in this group are...
- Get my work done
- Report to my boss
-

Example Map of Moral Communities

Your Map

Group: _____

This group's priorities are...

- _____
- _____
- _____

My roles in this group are...

- _____
- _____
- _____

Group: _____

This group's priorities are...

- _____
- _____
- _____

My roles in this group are...

- _____
- _____
- _____

You

Group: _____

This group's priorities are...

- _____
- _____
- _____

My roles in this group are...

- _____
- _____
- _____

Group: _____

This group's priorities are...

- _____
- _____
- _____

My roles in this group are...

- _____
- _____
- _____

Map of Your Moral Communities

You may have experienced many different reactions to this exercise. It may have been hard for you to put into words the things that have gone unspoken. It may also have been painful to explore the impact of the morally injurious event on your relationships and community. Perhaps you felt like avoiding others or stopping activities you once found meaningful. Although challenging, an essential part of using ACT to heal from moral injury is to notice and reflect on the experience of this pain. In taking time to reflect on the moral pain you have experienced, you are doing the opposite of avoidance; you are approaching the pain and discomfort that lie beneath your moral injury. By choosing to approach the pain, you are beginning to end the negative downward spiral of moral injury created and sustained by avoidance.

Summary

If moral injury is essentially a social wound, then healing from moral injury is ultimately a social process too. By mapping out your moral communities in this chapter, you have begun to identify the impact of the injury on your relationships with others and yourself. This insight allows you to begin the process of moral healing. (For extra practice read and complete the worksheet Mapping Your Moral Communities downloadable at http://www .newharbinger.com/44772.)

The remainder of this book will help you learn to use ACT techniques and skills to embrace the values—the things that matter to you—that will help you increase a sense of peace and purpose within yourself and toward the communities you care about. We will begin this journey by continuing to look at your relationship with yourself, working together to observe that you are much more than your thoughts, emotions, and memories—even much more than your moral injury. Let's journey forward.

PART 2

Embracing Moral Pain to Engage Moral Values

CHAPTER 4

You Are More Than You Know

All the world's a stage,
And all the men and women merely players;
They have their exits and their entrances;
And one man, in his time, plays many parts.

—William Shakespeare, *As You Like It*

In the previous chapter, we talked about how human morality is deeply intertwined with social relationships. Being a part of these relationships and communities means navigating different social roles and expectations, all of which may be impacted by moral injury. Now let's go beyond those roles and look at a *sense* of you that is more than the roles you experience in your life; indeed, more than *any* of your experiences—thoughts, feelings, sensations, memories, *and* social roles.

We chose that quote from Shakespeare very intentionally—because *you* are also like a stage. You are a place where many emotions and thoughts make their entrances and exits. You will have many roles to play in your life—some just once, others as long as you live. Recognizing this allows you to observe the many "plays" of your life, not getting so engrossed in just one role that it becomes the only one you ever play.

Let's begin by exploring what it means to have a self.

You as a Place Called Self

As we pointed out in the previous chapter, when people talk about what it is like to be "themselves," they often use labels to describe who they are, what they do, and how they behave. However, there is another amazing thing that human beings can do. We not only understand what we say; we also can notice that we are saying it. Humans are conscious and aware beings; we can observe changes in thoughts, feelings, and sensations as they make their entrances and exits—as they flow in and out of our experience. You can observe your experience. Having this knowledge can help you to change the way you relate to what you are saying, feeling, and sensing. This is an important part of moral healing.

Learning about how you relate to yourself, through becoming aware of your experiences, can help you to see if you are fused or entangled with any particular social role—like being a character stuck on the stage in the middle of a play. It can also help you notice if you are able to *observe* a character—as if you *are* the stage, gently holding the characters as they finish their lines before they exit. If you are the stage holding each character as they make their entrances and exits, then let's give this stage a name. For our purposes, we will call the stage, this larger sense of you, *self*. To continue this journey of knowing the self, complete this simple exercise.

Exercise 4.1: Twenty Statements

The following exercise is a variation of the Twenty Statements Test developed by Kuhn and McPartland (1954). To complete the exercise, fill in the blanks on the twenty lines that follow with a statement that is true for you. Examples include "I am the loneliest person I know," "I am broken beyond repair," and the like. Consider including the social roles that you identified in the exercises in chapter 3 and the labels you have for yourself concerning your moral injury (like *broken, damaged, unforgivable*). Take all the time you need to come up with twenty.

1. I am _____

2. I am _____

3. I am _____

4. I am _____

5. I am _____

6. I am _____

7. I am _____

8. I am _____

9. I am _____

10. I am _____

11. I am _____

12. I am _____

13. I am _____

14. I am _____

15. I am _____

16. I am _____

17. I am _____

18. I am _____

19. I am _____

20. I am _____

Review the labels you've given yourself, and notice what remains the *same* in every statement: the words "I am." No matter what you filled in, there is always an "I" that experiences each of those twenty roles or states of being. This "I" is the self that has each of these experiences, including moral injury.

Let's learn more about this self—this larger sense of self that holds each of your experiences and is also much more than those experiences.

Understanding the Self

You experience your sense of self in three distinct ways:

- Self-as-concept—the different characters on the stage

- Self-as-process—the movement of the characters on the stage, their entrances and exits

• Self-as-context—the stage itself, the sense of you that holds all the characters

Let's further define each of these senses of you and link them to moral injury and how recognition of these senses of self can help you to heal.

Self-as-Concept

Self-as-*concept* refers to the way you describe yourself. It includes each of the labels, ideas, and stories that you have about yourself. It is all of the characters on your stage. It includes the twenty statements you wrote in the preceding exercise as well as each of your social roles and identities. This "narrower" sense of self is reflected in answers you might give to the question, "Who are you?"

You might answer this question in many ways. You might describe yourself with descriptors like "smart," "strong," "weak," or "cowardly." You might answer with full stories about yourself that include things that have happened to you in the past or ideas about what you want in the future. We most often talk about our self-as-concept as our "identities."

Interestingly, the origin of the word *identity* is a word meaning the "same" or "oneness." Therefore, when we speak about our identities, we are saying that we are the same as the words we say about ourselves. *We treat the self and the words as equal.* We become one with our words. There is one very big problem with this: the descriptions and the thing described are two *different* things.

When we lose the distinction between thinking (the description) and the self who is doing the thinking, we become entangled with the words, descriptions, and labels our minds have learned about us. In your recovery from moral injury, recognizing self-as-concept is about disentangling self and mind; that is, disentangling who you are from the labels you use to define yourself—especially the negative ones linked to the moral injury (for example, "evil" or "broken"). You are a human being *with* a mind, not a human who *is* a mind. You are a self with concepts, identities, and social roles; you are not the identities and social roles themselves. Let's look at the process of disentangling the self from ideas and labels.

DISTINGUISHING THE SELF FROM CONCEPTS OF THE SELF

Think about the first exercise in this chapter, with the multiple descriptions of the "I." Now imagine that we have asked you to complete a list of two thousand descriptions rather than twenty. It would take a while to complete the list, but you could do it. And even two thousand words could not fully capture the essence of you. Even twenty thousand couldn't get to all that you are. In fact, the whole lifetime of stories you have about yourself can't capture the full essence of you.

It's a challenge to fully grasp that we are more than the words and stories we say about ourselves. We are so used to talking about ourselves that the words we use and the person using them seem to be the same. In other words, we get emotionally and intellectually attached to our labels and identities.

Getting attached to certain labels and identities isn't always a problem. It can sometimes be helpful to attach to certain identities or roles in one's life. For example, being in the role of a parent when you have children is important. But letting go of that role when you are on a date with your spouse might also be helpful. This simple example illustrates a key aspect of living well: being able to zoom out and notice your whole self when any one role or identity is causing stress or actual suffering in your life. At these times it is important to distinguish yourself from these labels, roles, and identities.

SELF-AS-CONCEPT AND MORAL INJURY

You need to see yourself as more than your labels, roles, and identities to be able to see that these do not define you. They are a *part* of your experience, but not the *whole* of your experience.

Particularly when part of your experience is the intense pain and suffering of moral injury, it can be hard to observe the parts of your experience that exist outside of that pain and your struggle with it. Recognizing that you are more than the words you (or others) use to describe you is just one step in this journey. So we invite you to continue even if right now your mind is questioning or even doubting the path ahead. Let's try this out by practicing distinguishing yourself from your words and ideas about yourself. In this exercise, you'll return to Exercise 4.1 or your list of twenty statements.

Exercise 4.2: Twenty Experiences That I Have

Read back through your twenty statements completed in Exercise 4.1. This time, as you read, instead of saying "I am [whatever you added to fill in the blank]," read each one using these words instead: "I am a person who experiences [whatever you added]." So, for example, instead of reading "I am broken" or "I am a father," read it as "I am a person who experiences brokenness" or "I am a person who experiences fatherhood." Take a moment to read each of these out loud.

Once you have finished reading the twenty statements from this new perspective, reflect on these questions:

1. When you read the statements this new way, do you notice more of a distinction, distance, or separation between the person ("I" or "self") and the words?

2. Where your words or labels include moral evaluations (like "bad"), did you notice these as experiences the self was experiencing—like a character moving onto and then off the stage? Notice how thoughts like these come and go and then come and go again.

3. Where the words or labels included social roles or expectations (like "father," "veteran," "nurse"), did you notice the distinction between the words and the person ("I")?

4. Again, notice the one thing that remains the same—the "I."

Even as we ask you to notice a sense of self that is more than any words or ideas, we also acknowledge that these words and ideas are there, and they play important roles in your life. To begin healing, it will be important to notice the distinction between self and descriptions of self and to disentangle yourself from the words or labels your mind generates when that entanglement interferes with living your values-based life. Even if "bad" is a label that you notice, it is important to recognize that a word like "bad" and yourself are two different things. "Bad" may be a character that crosses your stage, but it doesn't define you.

Self-as-Process

Self-as-process is the sense of you as a being who is constantly experiencing changes across time. As we've said, there are many plays on the stage; characters are coming and going and moving about the stage all the time. This is self-as-process. This self notices what's happening within and *around* you in the present moment. This self notices *change* across time. It is from this sense of self that you observe the *flow* of thoughts, emotions, and sensations as they rise and fall with each passing moment.

Self-as-Process and Moral Injury

When a person experiences moral injury, their struggle with moral pain can seem ever present. They can lose contact with the ongoing flow of experience and get stuck in one experience—the pain. They then begin to suffer as they either make great efforts to get rid of the pain or resign themselves to thinking they deserve the pain.

So we humans not only "buy" that we are the things we say about ourselves, but we can also lose sight of the fabric of our life as it is being continually woven. In this stuck place, it is as if the moral injury and the self are one, and the flow of experience has vanished. Most or many things in life then seem to get connected to the moral injury in some way. Whatever you do, wherever you go, the injury comes along, haunting you and impacting your relationships, your experiences, and your world.

Reconnecting to Self-as-Process with Mindfulness

So how do you reconnect with this sense of self-as-process when you've become entangled in concepts—labels, judgments, identities, and roles? *Mindfulness* is a tool you can use to strengthen your ability to simply notice—rather than become one with—the labels and ideas you have about yourself. Mindfulness allows you to connect to self-as-process. You connect to a sense of self that *observes the flow* of experiences, including the rise and fall of the emotions, thoughts, and sensations related to moral injury. The "stage" is mindful to the exits and entrances of the actors and the flow of the play as it unfolds.

Jon Kabat-Zinn (2009) defines mindfulness as "paying attention, on purpose, in the present moment and nonjudgmentally." Practicing mindfulness builds the ability to be aware and to notice the experiences that are happening in the here and now. Redirecting your attention in this way pulls you out of the past and the future, connecting you to what is happening in this moment, which is constantly shifting with the ongoing flow of experiencing. Developing this process of intentional, nonjudgmental awareness is essential for moral healing.

That said, just as the health benefits of physical exercise don't happen with a single trip to the gym, you can experience the benefits of mindfulness only through regular practice. Research shows that mindfulness helps decrease emotional reactivity and allows us to disengage from emotional pain. The use of mindfulness is also associated with greater awareness of positive emotions and more flexibility in thinking (Davis & Hayes, 2011). Developing the ability to simply notice your thoughts, emotions, and other experiences—to notice how each one rises and then falls—will allow you to notice that the experience of moral pain *isn't* ever present. An endless number of experiences are there to be sensed in the ongoing flow of moments across time.

You can learn to practice mindfulness in a number of ways. Take a few minutes now to read through and try out the mindfulness exercise (adapted from Walser & Westrup, 2007) that follows.

Exercise 4.3: Mindful Breathing

Begin this exercise by finding a comfortable place to sit. Place your feet squarely on the floor and sit in an alert, but not rigid position. Let your arms and hands rest comfortably. Then read the instruction in each bullet point and complete the mindfulness exercise. Spend forty-five to sixty seconds completing each bulleted task. It may help to set a timer.

1. Start by noticing that you can feel yourself sitting on the chair. Take time to become aware of each part of your body that is touching the chair, simply noticing each of the sensations.

2. Now turn your attention to the feeling of your feet on the floor. Just notice the sensations that you feel as your feet rest on the floor.

3. Now turn your attention to your body temperature. Are parts of you either warm or cold? Be aware of these sensations.

4. Shift your attention to your hearing. One by one, pay attention to each of the sounds that you hear. Simply notice all the different sounds around you.

5. Now bring your attention to your nose, and notice the sensation of air moving in and out. Simply notice your breathing, gently paying attention to the air coming in and flowing out.

6. Finally, release your attention from your breathing and again focus gently on your body and how it feels to sit in the chair. Sit quietly for a moment, noticing this experience, before moving forward in the workbook.

Mindfulness practice will help you to create space in your life for something more than moral pain. It connects you to a sense of you that is in motion—you are an experiencing being, not a static being. Becoming aware of *self-as-process* through mindfulness will help you live more fully in the present. Being aware of the moment is a powerful release from the past and the future. But this takes practice. Consider setting aside time daily to develop this resource for meaningful living and for staying in touch with the ongoing flow of experience daily. We'll revisit this topic throughout this book, particularly in chapter 8. You can also check out the chapter 8 handout for additional practice and resources.

Self-as-Context

The distinction between self and mind (thinking) becomes particularly important when something happens in life that you don't like or care for—such as moral injury. When moral pain becomes one of the characters on your stage, it's essential to notice that you are far more than just this one character—this one piece of your life (though this may be challenging at first). This character may be very loud, it may speak frequently, and it seems to show up in every scene—moral injury can seem to take up the whole stage, like a one-person show. You, however, are far more than a one-person show. Connecting with this sense of self—this self that is more than any one character on the stage—can help you recognize that you are more than your emotions, thoughts, sensations, and memories. The "stage-level" sense of self is the *self-as-context*.

You Are More Than You Know

Self-as-context is the largest self. Indeed, we usually experience this sense of self as limitless. It's the part of you that has always been there and always will be throughout your life. This self includes, but is *more than,* each emotion, thought, sensation, and identity you have ever experienced. In a sense, self-as-context is the place where all those things have occurred.

We have been using the metaphor of a stage as representative of self-as-context. There is great power in connecting to this sense of self that is the stage for all your experiences. From this place, you can see that you—the stage—are not merely the characters or the play; rather, you "hold" them. You are not your emotions, thoughts, memories, or even your identities. You are the place where your emotions and thoughts occur over time.

From this perspective, you have freedom. You can be present to your experiences, without becoming those experiences or letting them overwhelm you.

This may seem impossible to you right now. Indeed, it can be difficult and requires ongoing engagement—but it is well worth the time and effort. Let's take a closer look.

Observing You

You can connect with self-as-context at any time to sense the limitlessness of you as observer of your own experience. You can see that you see; you can notice that you feel; you are aware that you think and remember and that you have identities and roles. This experience of being the observer is vast—it is awareness itself.

Connecting to a sense of you as the stage that holds all of your experiences (characters called emotions, thoughts, memories, and sensations) has a powerful outcome. If you *have* memories and feelings and roles—but you *are* more than them—then none of them, by themselves, define you or control you. Noticing this larger sense of you can help you experience the freedom to choose.

The next exercise will help you get connected to this larger sense of you.

Exercise 4.4: The Observer

Find a comfortable place where you can sit and write, undisturbed. Take a few moments to simply breathe deeply and slowly, then begin the exercise. Before you write any responses, first read the instructions from start to finish. Then complete each step in order before moving to the next step.

1. Start by noticing any sensations in your body: for example, an itch, tension, or pain. As each sensation rises into your awareness, acknowledge it and then let your awareness move on to the next sensation. That doesn't mean pushing the previous sensation away. It simply means being aware of the next sensation. After you notice four or five sensations, write them down here.

_____

_____

_____

_____

_____

Now notice that although you *have* sensations, you are not any single sensation; you are the place where sensations occur. Take a moment and consider the millions of sensations you have experienced across your lifetime—pleasant and unpleasant ones.

2. Notice and recall different emotions you've had today (enjoyable ones or uncomfortable ones). Write four or five of them down here. Notice and describe when and why you were feeling them.

_____

_____

_____

_____

_____

Now notice that you have emotions, but you are not any single emotion. You are the place where emotions occur. You are more than your emotions.

3. Recall three memories and briefly write them here:

    •   Memory from childhood: _____

    _____

    •   Memory from last year: _____

    _____

    •   Memory from yesterday: _____

    _____

Now notice that you have these memories, but you are not any single one of them. The childhood memory, the one from last year, the one from yesterday—you can "see" each, yet there are many more. Notice that you are more than any of the memories you have.

4. Take a minute or two and let your mind wander. Now notice all the different thoughts that went through your mind in that short period of time. Write some of the thoughts here.

_____

_____

_____

_____

_____

Notice that you have thoughts, but you are not any single thought. You are the place where thoughts occur. Consider the billions of thoughts that you may have had in your lifetime. You are constantly thinking, yet you are more than what you think.

Notice the different aspects of you that you just explored—sensations, emotions, memories, thoughts. Notice that, as you explored the different experiences, there was a self there noticing these different experiences—an observer.

Self-as-Context and Moral Injury

The sense of you that knows that you have thoughts, feelings, sensations, and memories—the observer you (self-as-context)—is larger than any single experience. There's a self there, and it's the same self you've been your whole life. This observer is vast and can hold each experience you have ever had or will ever have: the good and the bad, the joy and the pain. This sense of you can hold your moral pain as well. And just as the stage holds the characters, you can hold the memories, emotions, thoughts, and sensations that come along with the moral pain. You are not your moral pain. It is an experience that you have, not an experience that you have become.

The Impact of Moral Injury on Your Sense of Self

Morally injurious events often can fundamentally change how you think about yourself or others. As mentioned in chapter 3, morality is also deeply tied to a sense of who you are in relation to others. A person may think of themselves as a "team player" or a "peacemaker," and they may behave in ways that are consistent with these identities in social situations. Such labels describe qualities that they feel are part of their true self.

Consider some of the roles and identities you have for yourself in your social relationships. If you behave consistently with these labels in the contexts where they apply, things seem to be fine. However, if you notice that you are acting inconsistently with the labels you have for yourself, then you may think not only that you have betrayed your personal values but that you also have betrayed or abandoned your true identity. You may even come to think that the "you" that was originally there—before the morally injurious event—might be gone forever. We promise you that this is not the case.

Morally injurious events, by definition, involve deep discrepancies between values and the behavior of oneself or others. When there are discrepancies between who you believe you are and the actions you took during the morally injurious event, you may feel deep guilt and shame. When you see such discrepancies between the behavior you expected of others and what you actually see them do, you may feel deep anger and resentment. These emotions and judgments are so strong that they can easily overwhelm you. You can become absorbed by these experiences to a point that you feel like you are the very experiences (emotions, thoughts, and sensations) themselves. You can get caught up in the story, believing that you *are* the characters, and lose connection with the stage that holds them (self-as-context).

Let's take a closer look at how moral injury can impact the three senses of self by returning to Henry from chapter 1.

Recall that Henry had two different social roles in his story. Most immediately, Henry was a squad leader who'd been assigned a military mission. Within that role, he met military expectations and followed the rules in finding and capturing a known insurgent leader. From a military standpoint, Henry accomplished his mission. He should feel proud, right? Yet Henry was haunted because of his second role—that of a father. While capturing the insurgent, Henry also took away the protector of a family that was not unlike his own. He watched that man's children screaming in terror and the man's wife crying in fear for what would become of her husband and her family.

When Henry returned home to his own family after deployment, he was reminded of this event every time he looked at his own children. He was tormented by judgments of himself as a "family destroyer" and "undeserving of a family of his own," given what he had done. The moral pain of these ideas and labels caused him to withdraw from his family. He began staying out late at night and drinking heavily. This created tensions in his marriage and distance between him and his children.

Henry got stuck in *self-as-concept*. He became so attached to the moral evaluations (like "destroyer") connected to the morally injurious event that he started to avoid—not wanting to continue to destroy. He became focused on finding ways to avoid being reminded of the event, sinking ever deeper into the idea that he was destructive. He engaged in activities designed to control his emotional pain. He withdrew from his family and drank excessively. He was stuck in the storyline of moral injury, playing the same character on stage every day and night.

If Henry could contact his *self-as-process*, he could become aware that his value of caring for and protecting family (the value that was violated) was still present and available to him within his family. He could notice that reacting to his moral pain by withdrawing from his family moved him away from that value rather than toward it. Connecting to self-as-process could assist him in observing the ongoing flow of thoughts, feelings, sensations, and memories, helping him get unstuck from the idea about himself ("I am a destroyer") that he was attached to. Contacting his *self-as-process* could help him to open up to other characters, have a more flexible stage presence, and allow other characters to move on and off the stage.

Contacting his *self-as-context* could help Henry become aware that he is more than his pain and the memory of the event. He could contact a larger sense of himself—the sense of him that is the stage and holds the characters but is not the characters. He would have thoughts about being a destroyer—these would come and go, but many other characters would be there to be experienced. Henry could hold the pain while still having the freedom to make choices that are consistent with his values. He could choose to be caring toward and protect his family. Engaging in these actions could also provide Henry with a renewed sense of pride and feelings of love that stand alongside the pain from his past.

Summary

In this chapter, we aimed to broaden your awareness of the different aspects of yourself—to realize that *you are more than you know*. If your idea of who you are is determined by the words in your mind—words describing your memories, emotions, and sensations—then you can become stuck within a limited sense of self. Finding and exploring your larger self-as-context (which is experienced as limitless) can open you to the space where you can make choices about your actions and what is most important to you. From this perspective— observing experience across time as well as through the sense of the unlimited self—you can be truly free to achieve the things that matter most to you. You can see that you are not limited by your moral injury or the things you tell yourself. (For extra practice, read and complete the worksheet You are More Than You Know downloadable at http://www.new harbinger.com/44772.)

The chapters that follow will explore more deeply the ways in which people get stuck following a moral injury. We will further discover how to get unstuck from this kind of pain, helping you to create a future about well-being and living well.

CHAPTER 5

Stepping Back from Judgments, Stories, and Rules

I used to think that the brain was the most wonderful organ in my body...and then I remembered who was telling me this.

—Emo Philips

In chapter 4, we worked on increasing awareness that you are much more than you may know. You discovered a larger sense of you and worked through different exercises to expand your understanding of yourself as an experiencer of emotion, thoughts, and sensations. In this chapter, you'll continue to build this sense of yourself as we help you recognize that you are a person *with* a mind rather than a person who *is* their mind.

Breaking Free from Struggling with Your Mind

In chapter 2, we briefly introduced the process of *defusion*—the main strategy in ACT for breaking free from the constant chatter going on in your mind. Defusion is about *stepping back* from thoughts and judgments and the painful struggles that we get into with these experiences. It can help us to notice the labels that we place on others and ourselves and, when needed, to "peel them off." Conversely, *fusion* with thoughts happens when we get so caught up in our stories, thoughts, expectations, and judgments that we miss the important distinction between the words and the thing or person those words are referring to, and we treat the word and the object as one and the same.

Because our minds are always with us, constantly chattering (try to not have a thought, and you will see what we mean), it can be all too easy to become fused with our thoughts.

With fusion, it seems like our thoughts are all-encompassing, defining our very being. Simply stated, we *become* our minds. We lose contact with the larger sense of self that is a thinking, feeling, sensing being. Instead, we are engulfed in the words of the mind. When we become fused with our minds in this way, we lose perspective on thinking (words), which, in turn, limits our choices (actions). If our mind says *go*, we go. If our mind says *don't go*, we don't go. If our mind says something is good, we treat it as good. And if our mind says something is bad, we treat it as bad. And on and on it goes.

The problem is, our minds sometimes view the world and ourselves with limited perspective, from only one angle. Our minds can be more efficient than effective. Our minds have many tools for efficiency—sayings, rules, and other mental shortcuts. While this is often extremely helpful, when we blindly follow our mind down these set paths, it can also lead us into some painful places. When we view things only one way, or look at the same thing over and over, playing it again in our head, it's easy to become fused with it, to assume that's just how it is and always will be. Defusion helps us to step back from our minds and get a 360-degree perspective on the issue at hand.

The "Am" in I Am

Have you ever made a mistake and reactively exclaimed, "I am stupid!"? This phrase leaves little space between "I" and "stupid." Moreover, the little word in between there, "am," promotes fusion. "Am" is the present tense of "to be." "Am" appears to define one's existence. So, saying "I *am* stupid" suggests that "stupid" defines your existence. Remember how you completed the Twenty Statements exercise in chapter 4? Fusion with labels and judgments can get you stuck, seeing yourself from only one perspective. But you are much more than any label you have for yourself.

You, like all of us, have probably done things that might be called "stupid." However, *you* are not stupid. Your existence is not stupid. Similarly, you are not "broken," "useless," "hopeless," "evil," "bad," or any of those other words your mind has used to label you since your morally injurious event. Defusion is important here. Taking a different view of your thinking can be helpful. By taking a step back from these words, labels, and judgments, we can begin to notice that there is a lot more going on around them.

To demonstrate, let's look at how fusion makes certain thoughts bigger, sometimes so big that they are the only things we notice. While we're doing that, we'll also invite you to notice what happens to the space around you when you get so close to your thoughts that you become entangled in them.

Exercise 5.1: There Is More Than You're Thinking

Begin by reading this paragraph all the way through; then engage in the activity. If you can, raise this book with both hands to eye level with your arms extended out in front of you, as if you are holding the book at a distance to read it. Focus your attention on the word "ENTANGLED" and then slowly bring the book toward your face until it's touching your nose. Pause for a moment, holding the book at your nose, and then slowly move the book away from your face until your arms are fully extended again. Do this a few times as you continue to focus on the word.

ENTANGLED

Once you are finished, answer the following questions:

1. What did you notice as you decreased the distance between you and the word "ENTANGLED"? What did you notice with the book pressed up against your face? Did you experience any sensations or emotions as you held the book in close?

_____

_____

- You likely noticed that "ENTANGLED" became bigger and the other text around it became fuzzy and impossible to read.

- You may have even stopped noticing that there were any other words around "ENTANGLED."

- When the book was touching your face (as if fused to it), you might have felt blocked, stuck, trapped, or restricted.

2. What did you notice changing as you increased the distance between you and "ENTANGLED"? What did you notice as you held the book away from yourself? Did you experience any sensations or emotions as you held the book farther away?

_____

_____

- You likely noticed that "ENTANGLED" became smaller and that the words around it came into clearer view.

- You may have even noticed that there was a whole world going on around the book.

- As you moved the book away, you may have felt more free, unrestricted, clear, or open.

3. What stayed the same, regardless of how close you were to the book?

_____

_____

- You likely noticed that "ENTANGLED" was always there, even though its size changed.

- Based on our discussion from the previous chapter, you may have also noticed that *you* were always there observing that you were thinking.

This exercise is meant to convey an essential message: when we are fused with a thought, we have less room to see other things going on around that thought, which leads to less freedom to *do* other things. We do recognize the difficulty of defusing; after all, your mind is always present. It may be especially difficult when these thoughts are moral judgments connected to immensely painful moral emotions such as shame or hatred. Let's keep moving forward, though, with the goal of demonstrating how defusion may help you gain the freedom and flexibility needed to make changes in your life.

Finding Freedom by Gaining Distance

The goal of defusion is to gain enough distance from your thoughts that you can also see what else is going on within and around you. Then, from this place of observation, you can determine the direction you want to go in, the choices you want to make, and the actions you want to take. When we get too entangled in our thoughts and bogged down in our feelings, we become stuck. Defusion helps us become unstuck. *Sometimes* gaining a more distanced perspective allows us to notice something we hadn't noticed before.

Defusion Does Not Make Thoughts Disappear

It is important to know that defusion from thoughts doesn't make the thoughts go away. As you noticed in exercise 5.1, even when you held the book at a distance, the word "ENTANGLED" remained on the page. This is also the case for many of your labels and evaluations. Even when you begin to step back from your thoughts, they don't disappear. Thoughts of being wrong or bad may remain; stepping back brings freedom from entanglement, but not necessarily freedom from the labels themselves. Freedom, however, buys you options, whereas entanglement keeps you stuck.

So how do we deal with the evaluative and judgmental words that our minds say about us? When it comes to the painful reality of past moral violations, we may need to shift our *stance* toward these thoughts. This stance requires willingness or acceptance. We introduced the importance of this stance in chapter 2 and will explore it more in chapter 7. Practicing defusion from an open and accepting stance will assist when the thoughts and feelings of past moral violations arise.

Defusion helps guide us to a place of freedom. From this place, we can:

- Have difficult thoughts.

- Notice that they come and go.

- Move in a freely chosen and values-aligned direction *even with* these thoughts flowing through our mind.

Another aspect of defusion involves taking evaluative and judgmental words less literally. That doesn't mean disregarding what's true. You can acknowledge truth—the painful reality of a moral violation—but also acknowledge the words in your mind for what they are: simply words. Remember, our minds sometimes prioritize efficiency over effectiveness. They tend to take words at face value—making things easier, faster. Through the process of defusion, we notice that words have meanings, yet the words themselves are only words. They have no physical form; they can't be touched, tasted, or smelled. You could even say that they are just scribbles written on a page or sound vibrations in the air. Most important, they don't literally exist in you (or others).

Let's try another exercise to demonstrate how, when we buy into what our minds are saying, we can lose sight of the distinction between words and what the words refer to.

Exercise 5.2: "Lemons" Are Not Lemons

The exercise should take three to five minutes. We invite you to take a closer look at the words written on this page. If you are able, read these instructions aloud as you go, so that you can hear the words as well. Read and speak slowly, really taking your time to notice each of the experiences you will be asked to focus on.

1. Place this book in front of you, on a table or desk or on your lap, so that your hands are free.

2. Imagine you have a fresh lemon in your hands. You've just picked it off a tree. Notice how the lemon *looks:* its vibrant yellow color, its oval shape, the small dimples in the skin. Take time to really see every aspect of this lemon in your hands.

3. Now, imagine the way the lemon *feels.* Feel the texture—smoothness or roughness—of the skin as you move your fingers over it. Squeeze the lemon or press into it with your thumb and notice whether it is firm or squishy. Notice the weight and how it feels as you roll it back and forth in your hands.

4. Next, imagine taking your fingernails and digging them into the skin of the lemon, breaking it open. Notice the *sound* that the skin makes as you break through. Begin to pull the lemon apart slowly and notice the sound that it makes as you tear it open. Keep slowly pulling the lemon apart, listening closely, until you have broken it in two.

5. Imagine bringing one half of the lemon up to your face and inhaling deeply through your nose, paying attention to the *scent* of the lemon. Imagine its tangy aroma. As you smell the fragrant tartness of the lemon, notice if your mouth begins to water.

6. Finally, bring one half of the lemon slowly to your mouth and take a big bite, *tasting* the fruit. Notice your reactions: your lips may pucker, you may feel a pinch in your jaw, you may scrunch up your face. Even as these things happen, continue to chew the lemon slowly, and notice its taste.

7. Now come back to reading and explore the following reflection:

Reflection: In the past few minutes, you have seen, felt, heard, smelled, and tasted a lemon. But are you actually holding a lemon? Chances are there's not a lemon anywhere near you. And yet, by connecting fully with the words on this page and the imagery in your mind, you were reacting—seeing the lemon, salivating, tasting, and scrunching up your face. You were reacting to an image that your mind created. However, there is no lemon, only the word "lemon" and your reactions to it.

8. Now, take a moment to think about the evaluative and judgmental words you use to describe yourself and/or others who may have harmed you. Some of these might have already shown up in the Twenty Statements exercise in the previous chapter. Write some of these words in the space below. Take a little time with each. Notice how you feel as you write them.

_____

_____

_____

_____

_____

_____

_____

What emotions do these words evoke in you? What feeling do you get in your body? Maybe a heaviness, or a sharp pain, or the strong urge to get up and move away. As you did with the lemon, by fully connecting with these words—fusing with them—you're reacting. But remember, you weren't literally holding a lemon just because you thought about a lemon. And you aren't literally broken, bad, or evil just because your mind "holds" those thoughts.

Because you've tasted a lemon, your mind can recreate that taste. If you once felt broken or once experienced a moral violation (something "bad"), your mind can recreate that experience too. In this way, you can taste a lemon that's no longer there, and you can experience a sense of "brokenness" or "badness" when the violation is in the past.

If at this point you're noticing something within you pushing back, this could be your mind. Or maybe it's your heart; the pushback may be beyond the words in your mind, and you *feel* the truth of these painful moral judgments. We want to recognize that this pain is real. The key message in this exercise is about recognizing the distinction between *words* and what they refer to. Because we think in words and images, we treat them as if they are literally true and present. But this can get us stuck in moral pain. As we journey forward, we'll return to this felt sense of moral truth—the one that comes from the heart. For now, we invite you to continue on this portion of our journey: defusing from your mind.

Taking Back Power from Words

Human language is amazing. Our verbal abilities allow us to communicate in complex ways with others and with ourselves. The dark side of language arises when we overestimate the power of language to control our inner experience. When we try to use the power of words to control the uncontrollable, suffering is inevitable. In the next few sections, we'll look at some of the most common—and most painful—ways that language can promote fusion and create suffering, seemingly taking away your power of choice. We'll emphasize how each of these pitfalls can turn natural moral pain into suffering.

Describing Versus Evaluating

Let's start by looking at the difference between describing and evaluating. *Describing* involves using information gathered with our five senses to give a verbal account of the characteristics or qualities of something or someone. Describing relies on facts, verifiable in the real world, and does not include opinions, assumptions, or judgments. *Evaluating* involves determining the importance, value, usefulness, or worth of something or someone. It relies on personal judgment and is often subjective, involving opinion. Evaluation also often leads to comparison and labeling of things or people. Judgments can be painful, and fusion with these words can lead to suffering.

Before diving into the pitfalls of evaluation, let us clarify: we're not saying evaluation is always bad. That would be a judgment in and of itself, which would be inflexible and unhelpful. Indeed, some judgments are quite useful. Evaluative words, though, do tend to be rather "sticky" and are much easier to fuse with.

Exercise 5.3: Sticky Words

The following list includes several evaluative words that show up in moral injury. Place a check mark next to the ones that you've noticed yourself struggling with. If there are other, similar evaluation words you've noticed that aren't included here, add those in the blank spaces and check them off as well.

- ☐ Bad
- ☐ Wrong
- ☐ Corrupt
- ☐ Monstrous
- ☐ Worthless/useless
- ☐ Worst
- ☐ Disgusting
- ☐ _____

- ☐ Evil
- ☐ Unforgivable/irredeemable
- ☐ Tainted/stained
- ☐ Horrible/horrific
- ☐ Immoral
- ☐ Ruined
- ☐ Broken
- ☐ _____

Review the words you checked. See if you can detect what we mean by "sticky." These types of words tend to pull people in, like quicksand. We get caught up in them and struggle, as they seem to tell us that we are somehow broken and need fixing. They can even sink us into darker places, where we feel we don't deserve love or kindness, or even to be a part of humanity. These words seem to be especially powerful.

We want to lessen that power of words through defusion—making them less sticky, and giving you back the freedom to move forward.

Evaluation Takes Us Out of the Present Moment

One big problem with evaluation is that it tends to take us out of the present moment—the here and now. In chapter 8 we will talk at length about the importance of living in the present moment. For now, we just want to note how evaluation problematically transports us across time and space. Let's explore how defusion through *non*evaluative description can help you to stay grounded in the here and now.

Have you ever said to yourself, "If only I were young again, life would be so much better" or "Once I get a little older, everything will be great"? These are natural and common statements. With respect to the morally injurious event, have you ever said to yourself, "If only that had never happened, everything would be better"? This, too, is a natural statement that anyone might say following a moral violation.

If this last statement resonated with you, your mind likely had several follow-up comments. Maybe it had some judgments about how good things might have been and how bad things are. If you do notice any of those, jot them down here:

_____

_____

_____

Exploring whether these thoughts are helpful to you right now, in this moment, can be useful. Our goal is not to debate the truth or untruth of these thoughts, but rather to see how they work in your life.

When the mind gets wrapped up in judging the past or future, in judging oneself or others, it's not paying attention to the moment. While the mind is busy *imagining* how great it would be if it weren't for a particular event or memory, or when it's *dwelling* on a past choice, we relinquish our power to *do* anything right now, in this moment. As a result, we've also given away another precious here-and-now moment that we can never get back.

See if you can observe what you wrote with some distance, getting space between you and your evaluations.

Evaluation Leads to Reason-Giving

Evaluation can also lead to another barrier to vital living—reason-giving. Our logical minds deduce or infer reasons from our evaluations and conclusions. This can be helpful when it leads us toward a richer life. For example, you could conclude that because the sunset was so beautiful last time you watched it, you want to go see it again. Your reason for wanting to go see the sunset a second time is that you evaluated it as beautiful last time. However, the darker side of language can lead us to use our more problematic evaluations as reasons for moving *away* from meaningful connections and vital living. If, because of your past actions, you judge yourself as a bad person, you might conclude that you don't deserve love from others. Based on this conclusion—this reason—you might withdraw from relationships and isolate yourself. This sort of evaluation and reason-giving turns pain into suffering.

Using the process of defusion, you can notice that reasons, too, are just words. Reasons themselves are not causes. Beautiful sunsets don't *cause* us to go see them again. We *choose* to go see them again. And negative evaluations don't cause us to isolate or pull away from things that matter. The words—thought, spoken, or written—cannot literally cause the action. Defusing from reasons gives us the space we need to choose the most meaningful course of action.

Storytelling Seems Powerful

Storytelling is one special way of using language. Stories are an important part of almost every culture and community around the world. Storytelling appears to have happened in one form or another since the very beginning of human language. Indeed, stories are an efficient and effective method for communicating across time and space. Stories are convenient, powerful tools for organizing important information. We each carry many different stories.

Noticing Our Moral Stories

There are many kinds of stories, but since this book is about healing from moral injury, let's look specifically at moral stories—those that tell the tales of our communities and our values and relationships within these communities. They tell us how our communities operate—what is the right thing to do and what is the wrong thing to do. Any story that has a "good guy" and a "bad guy" has a moral component to it. In these stories, good guys are good because they do the right things, and bad guys are bad because they do the wrong things.

When we step right up next to these stories—and even enter them—it becomes very easy to fully embrace the labels of bad or good. Think about your favorite book or movie with a villain—a bad guy—whom you dislike or hate. Notice how you can get caught up in the morality of their behavior. Notice that you have real feelings and real reactions to them.

Now, if we're talking about a book or a movie, this kind of fusion can be okay. It can help us get better connected with the story and increase the excitement of the emotional roller coaster that a great book or movie can take us on. But if we're talking about our own life stories, the ones about our own traumas, betrayals, and injuries, then fusion—getting *into* the story—can lead to struggles and suffering. When we dive into these stories, when we get inside them, we miss the larger—much larger—story of our lives. The one that's still happening right now, and will be happening still tomorrow, and the next day, and the next.

Trapped by Our Moral Stories

There are many reasons why the biggest movies in Hollywood have such courageous heroes and nefarious villains, and why many of the bestselling books are about epic battles between good and evil. These kinds of stories pull you in. For Hollywood, this is great, but for you, perhaps not. When you get pulled into your own moral stories, you may become trapped, fused inside the story. Defusion opens the door that leads you out of this trap. By stepping back from your moral stories, you can see these stories for what they are—events from the past that are *part* of your story, not your *whole* story. Morally injurious experiences are among the most painful of plot twists. And, indeed, they can effect a change in the course of your story. However, they—like any one story—will never be your whole story.

Moral Rules

Earlier in this book, we talked about morality of the mind, which includes all the thoughts we have about right and wrong, good and bad, just and unjust. These beliefs or expectations are learned from our communities—our families, friends, schools, faith communities, and so on. These beliefs are often summarized and organized into a string of words we call a "rule." Rules are defined as specific codes that govern the ways we should behave. Rules are shortcuts that guide behavior. Rules are designed to ensure that specific underlying values are not violated. However, they don't ensure that values are lived.

Governments have rules in the form of laws. Religious institutions have rules such as commandments or *mitzvot*. The military and law enforcement agencies have rules of engagement. Many of these are *moral rules*, which help to ensure that the desires or priorities of one individual or a small group do not negatively impact the larger community. In this way, rules can be extremely helpful and important.

Distinguishing Between Moral Rules and Moral Values

When we fuse with rules, though, our behavior can become rigid and inflexible, and our lives unworkable. Moreover, in the face of *broken* rules, we can get fused with a sense of *broken*-ness and begin grappling with questions of right and wrong, forgivability, and punishment. When we're fused with the rule, we may see no way out of a difficult predicament. And in the case of a past moral violation, we may see no way forward, instead experiencing ourselves as permanently disconnected ("broken") from the values from which the rules were born.

It is important, then, to distinguish rules from values. We briefly introduced values in previous chapters, and we'll explore values more in the next chapter. For now, we'll illustrate with an example. Let's explore the rule "Do not lie."

Rules set a boundary to keep us from violating our values. At its core, the rule "do not lie" keeps us from violating the broader values of honesty and integrity. Yet most of us simultaneously hold multiple values to guide our actions. Because rules are shortcuts, they can be problematic if we act on them inflexibly.

Imagine you've been invited to dinner at your friends' house. They cooked the meal. After the first several bites, you realize that it doesn't taste very pleasant. Nothing wrong with it; just rather bland. Your friend turns to you with a hopeful look and asks how you like the food. You respond with a smile: "It's wonderful; thank you for all your efforts preparing such a beautiful meal for us!" You've broken the rule "Do not lie" by implying to your friends that the dinner they prepared was delicious when, to you, it wasn't.

But why did you do this? Almost certainly because there were multiple values in play that influenced your relationship with your friends. Perhaps there was a value of honesty and integrity. However, there were additional values of kindness, caring, and support toward friends. In some circumstances it's not possible to fully express both sets of values in a single action. In that moment you chose to take a step back from the rule "Do not lie" and to prioritize caring and support over full honesty. You chose, instead, to express the values of caring by showing appreciation for the effort your friends had made on your behalf.

This may seem like a harmless example—one that certainly does not have the weight of a morally injurious event. A classic moral dilemma with a bit more heaviness may help to further illustrate.

Exercise 5.4: Flexibly Defusing from Moral Rules

Read the following short story (adapted from Kohlberg, 1981) and, in the space provided, briefly answer the questions.

A woman was on her deathbed. There was one treatment that might save her, a new medication that a doctor in the same town had recently discovered and patented. The drug was expensive to make, and the doctor was charging patients ten times what the drug cost him to produce. The sick woman's husband, Heinz, went to everyone he knew to borrow the money, but he could get only about half of what he needed. He told the doctor that his wife was dying and asked him to sell it cheaper or let him pay later. But the doctor said no. So Heinz got desperate and broke into the doctor's office to steal the medicine for his wife. After taking it, she made a full recovery.

1. Should Heinz have broken into the doctor's office to steal the medicine?

    Yes   No

2. Why or why not?

    _____

    _____

    _____

3. What values were expressed by Heinz's actions? What values were expressed by the doctor's actions?

    _____

    _____

    _____

4. What sorts of rules might have come into play as Heinz made his decision?

    _____

    _____

    _____

5. Now, whatever your initial answer was—yes or no—provide a potential argument for the *other* answer.

    _____

    _____

    _____

Whether you initially agreed or disagreed that Heinz should steal the medicine, you were likely able to come up with a logical argument both for and against. How did you do that? You must have stepped back far enough from whatever rules guided your original decision to notice the other potential options. If Heinz had been fused with a rule—for example, "Thou shalt not steal"—he might have perceived no real choice available to him. Or, if he chose to violate the rule, fusing with it after the fact, he might have concluded that he was a bad person for stealing. The main point here is that defusion allows us to consider all options and potentially prioritize our values—our guiding lights in life.

Prioritizing Moral Values over Moral Rules

Moral rules, whether they have been codified into laws, regulations, or doctrines, are generally intended to promote safety, health, and thriving of the community. However, as with other words, if we get stuck in those rules, we can lose freedom of choice and give away the ability to flexibly consider what it could mean for ourselves and others if those rules are broken. Rather than rigidly and inflexibly responding to rules, we advocate prioritizing values and acknowledging that multiple and sometimes conflicting values can be involved in any given situation. It's essential that we be able to flexibly examine a situation and make choices that may prioritize one value over another. Rules can be rigidly followed and possibly unhelpful in a particular context. For Heinz, desperate to save his wife's life yet trying to play by the rules, prioritizing his moral values might help him choose an action that is most aligned with his moral compass.

Values may transcend contexts. Prioritizing your most important values may allow you to find continuity and help you chart a way forward in the multiple contexts of your life. We'll spend the next chapter focusing on values, helping you to identify yours and how to bring them to life.

Summary: Creating Flexibility

As we near the end of this chapter, we want to circle back to the purpose of defusion. By stepping outside of our moral stories, stepping back from our judgments of ourselves and others, and defusing from moral rules, we give ourselves much-needed space. This space allows us the freedom to see and to choose. Even though, when we step back from "ENTANGLED," we notice that the evaluations and judgments are still there, stepping back still has value. There is a new space between you and your mind—and in that space there is freedom, opportunity, and hope. Freedom to behave in a new way. Opportunity to change the course of the story, the one unfolding right here and now. And hope for values-aligned living in this moment and each moment to come. (For extra practice read and complete the worksheet Stepping Back from Judgments, Stories, and Rules downloadable at http://www.newharbinger.com/44772.)

As you continue our journey of moral healing, you've now explored yourself as the context in which each of your experiences occurs. You have noticed that you are so much *more* than any one of those experiences—thoughts, feelings, or actions. You've also taken a step back from those experiences of mind and noticed that they are actually not what they pretend to be. The language of the mind is powerful, but it's a lot less powerful when we defuse: when we peek behind the curtain, seeing thinking for what it is and gaining freedom of choice. From here, we'll step into an exploration of values and the life-enriching choices available there.

CHAPTER 6

Values as the Flip Side of Moral Pain

What you do makes a difference, and you have to decide what kind of difference you want to make.

—Jane Goodall

Living life with purpose and meaning can sometimes prove challenging, especially when you feel captured by the pain of past events. In the previous chapter, we described how your mind is something that you *have*, not something that you *are*. We explored how you can defuse or gain some distance from your mind and thoughts in the service of taking important actions in your life today. In this chapter, we will explore what guides those important actions: values. We will work to help you clarify what those essential qualities of life are, helping you to discover (or rediscover) what matters most to you. We will also look at how values are connected to moral pain. Indeed, the pain you experience as a result of your morally injurious experience tells you what is important to you and may also reconnect you to what it means to be human.

Values: Your Personal Compass

In chapter 1, we briefly introduced values as the guiding lights that illuminate what is important to us as we travel the path of life. In chapter 2, we described how engagement with values gives life vitality and purpose, while disengagement from values leads to pain and potential suffering.

Let's start here by more clearly defining values. Values are broad, abstract principles that guide us in how we live; more specifically, they are personal or social standards of behavior that we follow to live a life of meaning.

It might be helpful at this point to distinguish values from goals. Goals are achievable. You can set a goal and accomplish it, but you never accomplish or achieve values; you can always continue to live by them in your life. Goals are like mile markers on the journey of life; you can reach one and then set out to reach another. Values are more like the compass pointing you in the direction in which you want to travel. Just as you could travel west forever, you can continuously move in the direction of your values. If being loving is your value, there is always more loving to do.

Values are deeply personal, so it's no wonder that we often choose to spend time with people with similar values. But even your spouse or your best friend is unlikely to have the exact same values prioritized in the exact same way as you do. Through awareness and the capacity to create our own meaning in our lives, we learn that we are each free to choose which values we will live by.

Lastly, personal values tend to not be situation specific. For example, someone who values *caring* is likely to act according to that value across most situations. Perhaps they do this by providing for their family, being there for their friends in times of need, volunteering at their church or for various causes, *and* serving well the people with whom they work. Certain values may move up or down the priority list depending on the specific situation, and perhaps some values may not apply to a specific situation. However, these important guiding principles tend to endure across most areas of our lives.

Moral Values: Your Moral Compass

As we discussed in chapter 3, moral values are those that connect us with others and serve to guide our actions in support of the greater community. Many people struggling with moral injury describe a feeling that their "moral compass is broken." They express this in a number of ways. For example, "Something is wrong with me (or others) because of what I (they) did" or "I am evil." Have you had any of these thoughts or something similar to them? If so, you're not alone.

Consider two important points. First, again, the fact that you experience moral pain does not mean that you are broken. Rather, it is a sign that your system for signaling and relaying information about moral violations is functioning. Your values compass is intact. If, however, you are suffering from moral injury, perhaps you are indeed "off course." You may no longer be following your values compass—but not because your compass is broken. Rather, you may have stopped moving forward in the direction your compass is pointing in. Has this happened for you? If yes, you may have avoided the path that you care about to avoid the experience of pain. But now you have become stuck, and your life journey is on hold.

It is possible, though challenging, to step back onto the path and move forward. Indeed, moving forward on your values-directed path is part of healing from moral injury. We're going to work together to help you clarify and engage your values, providing you with much-needed encouragement to move forward on your values-directed path.

Exercise 6.1: Identifying Your Values

In this exercise, we want to help you to identify and clarify your values, including some of your moral values. Start by reading through a list of values. Read the entire list before you complete the numbered steps at the end of the values list.

Acceptance	Equality	Industry	Romance
Adventure	Excitement	Intimacy	Safety
Assertiveness	Fairness	Justice	Self-awareness
Beauty	Fitness	Kindness	Self-care
Caring	Flexibility	Love	Self-control
Challenge	Freedom	Mindfulness	Self-development
Compassion	Friendliness	Open-mindedness	Sensuality
Conformity	Forgiveness	Order	Sexuality
Connection	Fun	Patience	Skillfulness
Contribution	Generosity	Persistence	Spirituality
Cooperation	Gratitude	Pleasure	Supportiveness
Courage	Honesty	Power	Trust
Creativity	Humility	Reciprocity	Other:
Curiosity	Humor	Respect	_____
Encouragement	Independence	Responsibility	Other: _____

1. Go back through the list and cross out any words that don't resonate with you—values that don't fit for you at this time. Crossing off values you don't share with others is okay.

2. Now go through what is left on the list and place a star or check mark to the left of the values that are of high importance in your life at this time. Mark as many as you'd like.

3. Next, rank-order your top five values, writing the numbers 1 through 5 to the right of the value. This may be challenging, as each value may seem as important as the others, but try to rank them anyway. Remember, your values are still there, even if you may not be living them in the way you would like. This is just a personal exploration exercise, and you are free to reevaluate or change your mind at any time.

4. Consider the definition of moral values—values that connect us with others and serve to guide our actions in support of the greater community—and underline those of your values that appear to be social. It's okay if you aren't sure. Consider the values instilled in you by influential people and communities in your life.

5. Finally, take a moment to consider the values that were violated, that led to your ongoing experience of pain and, in turn, led you to this book. See if those values are listed here—whether there are one or many, circle them.

6. Take a moment to reflect on this exercise. Were you surprised by anything? Did any emotions or thoughts show up about how you are living your values? Did any of them remind you of the moral injury? Write your reflections in the space provided.

_____

_____

_____

Bear in mind that right now, you are just clarifying your values and looking to see which may have been violated. This may be challenging, but hang in there. You can always return to living your values. That is a large part of what this book is about.

For some people, their values are clear and easy to identify; they may even be easy to rank-order. For others it is more difficult. We each have multiple deeply held values. Bringing your values into your awareness and clarifying them will make it easier to engage them in your day-to-day life.

As you worked through the exercise, you may have noticed that one or more of your values was violated during the morally injurious event. Keep these specific values in mind as you continue through this chapter, learning more about how violation of important values can lead to pain and even to great suffering. Ultimately, we want you to discover how reconnecting to values also gives hope and leads to healing.

Mind and Heart in Conflict

There are three ways that morality of the mind and of the heart can come into conflict, which may constrain the very values that ordinarily give life meaning and purpose.

This first way is when the heart and mind disagree. In some cases, a values violation includes an action or inaction that can be logically explained, yet still *feels* wrong and painful.

To further explore this idea, let's revisit the story of SGT Howell from the introduction. SGT Howell made a choice to shoot a child who was wearing an explosive vest and walking toward his fellow service members. According to the military's rules of engagement, SGT Howell acted appropriately. His rationale for firing made logical sense: "If I don't kill him, he will kill us." But if SGT Howell held values such as caring and kindness, taking the life of a child would be incredibly painful, even if the action was also logical. While his head told him that he did the right thing, his heart still ached with moral pain.

Check in with your experience of moral injury. Do you notice this sort of disagreement or struggle between your mind and your heart? Note, the struggle between mind and heart does not have to be as clear as in this example. Sometimes these types of struggles are more subtle.

Take a moment to reflect deeply and answer these questions:

What does your mind say about the violation of your values that happened in the morally injurious event? Can you logically work out the violation and why it happened? Do you have a thought or story that you or others have used to try to explain it?

_____

_____

_____

What does your heart say about the violation of your values that happened in the morally injurious event? What were and are your feelings about the violation of your values?

_____

_____

_____

The second way mind and heart may struggle is with moral dilemmas in which two or more moral values seem to conflict. For instance, there may be two "right" choices or two "wrong" choices. Remember Heinz in the previous chapter? He had the choice to steal the medicine for his wife, which would have been the "right" choice as it aligned with his value of caring for his loved ones, but stealing is illegal. He also had the choice not to steal the medicine, which would have been the "right" choice, as it aligned with his value of integrity, but his wife would have died. In an instance such as this, choosing one value means violating another. In a high-stakes situation, there may be painful consequences whichever choice is made.

The third way minds and hearts struggle often arises some time after the violation, when values prioritized in one community may not be prioritized in another. Actions previously considered "right" in one context may be considered "wrong" in another. This is most common when we make significant changes in our lives, like separating from the military and reintegrating into the civilian world, leaving a violent group or community, or joining a new faith community. After these moves, past actions that once made sense no longer do; this can lead to struggles connecting with the new community and relating to oneself.

Sometimes the mind and the heart _do_ agree. And what they agree on is the "wrongness" of the action or inaction. Then the mind and heart can band together to try and repair the violation. They can look for ways to restore the connection with those violated values. This might be through giving or seeking forgiveness or by making amends or seeking restitution. However, sometimes the mind and heart can also work together in a punishing way. In these cases of self-punishment, the mind and heart are _not_ in conflict, but moral injury may still arise if you become disconnected from your values in a way that magnifies pain and creates suffering. We'll describe this more following the next exercise.

In this section we've reviewed three ways whereby heart and mind can come into conflict or struggle in the aftermath of a moral violation. Experiencing such conflict can keep you stuck, preventing you from moving forward in life. One key to moving forward is strengthening your ability to notice the conflict, and then to decide what actions your most important values direct you to do in the here and now.

Exercise 6.2: Noticing the Conflict

This is a reflective writing exercise. We invite you to write freely about your experience of struggles between heart and mind concerning your values that were violated. As you do, complete the following:

1. Review the values you marked in Exercise 6.1 (values violated during the moral injury). Then consider the preceding descriptions about ways the mind and heart may (a) disagree with one another, (b) have to make an impossible choice between two important values, or (c) struggle with actions that once seemed to make sense but now do not.

2. Write here about how your struggle fits into one or more of these descriptions or how your experience feels different from any of them.

_____

_____

_____

_____

_____

_____

_____

It's important to examine how your heart and mind disagree. If that is the case, this may be contributing to the moral pain: your mind may be able to logically explain the action or inaction that caused the moral injury, yet in your heart it may *feel* wrong and painful.

Remember, heart and mind may agree or disagree, but you can hold both. You are more than any one of the experiences you have had. Also, keep in mind that none of the experiences of mind or heart need to be changed before you can reengage your values. This may seem impossible, but let's look more closely at what can happen following a morally injurious event. It isn't that values disappear; it's that they get lost in the pain and criticism.

Disconnecting from Values Due to Past Values Violations

Moral pain arises after a values violation precisely because of the disturbance in your relationship with that value. When a morally injurious event happens, you get knocked off the values path. But the compass isn't broken. As we've said, this difficult mental, emotional, and perhaps spiritual pain is an important signal that your actions or those of others have been inconsistent with what matters most to you. However, the ongoing suffering of moral injury is brought about *when you remain disconnected from these values over time.*

There may be many reasons someone stays disconnected from their values. We will describe the following four:

- Avoidance of painful reminders

- A sense of unworthiness

- Punishment of yourself or others

- Rigidity about values

There may be other reasons that someone stays disconnected, but these are the more common ones. As you read them, consider which may be affecting you; there may be more than one. Also, think about whether there are other reasons relevant to you that we may have missed. Regardless, notice how, inevitably, this separation from values and disengagement from values-aligned actions leads to suffering, sorrow, and a feeling that life is lacking in meaning.

Avoidance of Painful Reminders

People suffering from moral injury will often avoid the people, places, and activities connected with the violated values, because engaging with those things brings up painful thoughts, emotions, and sensations. Remember Mae, the firefighter who made the difficult decision to leave the burning apartment, unable to save the child? She felt immense regret and guilt, often feeling these emotions intensely when she remembered hearing the child crying in the burning room. Mae had two young children of her own around the same age as the child in the apartment. When they cried or screamed, even with excitement, she was struck by a deeply painful sense of guilt and regret, as it reminded her of the child who died that day.

Mae had joined the fire department because she held values of caring for and ensuring the safety of others. Again, our values tend to not be context specific; they inform our actions across many situations. Mae cares deeply for her children and wants to protect them. If, as a result of the moral injury, Mae begins to avoid her own children or to treat them harshly to keep them away from danger or away from her, she may be inadvertently stepping off the path of her values, which makes it more likely she will suffer further. Her efforts to avoid moral pain bring about additional pain. She has disengaged from how she would like to live her values, adding another layer of pain. This additional layer is suffering itself.

A Sense of Unworthiness

People may also become disconnected from values through a sense of unworthiness. We hinted at this previously when we described getting stuck in (or fused with) judgments. This kind of disconnection may include thoughts that we are unworthy of love, connection, happiness, success, freedom, or other values—usually when we feel we are responsible for the violation of our values.

Consider the story of Robert at the beginning of this book. His son died when Robert caused a car wreck by texting while driving. If Robert experiences immense self-blame and condemnation so that he develops a sense he is unworthy of the love and trust of his wife and remaining child, he may pull away from them. He may even actively push them away. In doing so, however, Robert is "losing" both of his children as well as his wife. So Robert's pain at the loss of his son, compounded by his sense of unworthiness and his withdrawal from his loved ones, brings further suffering and even greater loss. Not only will Robert continue to struggle, but his remaining child and his wife will miss out on his love and support at the time they are most needed. In a sense, by trying to avoid his pain, he's perpetuating the values violation.

Punishment of Yourself or Others

Sometimes disengagement from values can be used as a form of punishment. If your own actions caused the violation, you may deny yourself opportunities to engage in values-aligned behaviors. This may be connected with a thought that you no longer deserve the fruits of those values. Denying values engagement punishes you for the past violation. It may also end up punishing those closest to you. Again, this process perpetuates the pain.

Returning to Mae's story: from her perspective, her inaction resulted in the death of a child. And she experienced this as a violation of her duty as a firefighter and her values of caring for and protecting others. If, as the result of this painful experience, Mae were to quit the fire department as a way of punishing herself—denying herself future opportunities for active engagement with her values—she would likely experience more significant suffering. Worst of all, she would be denying herself opportunities for forgiveness, restitution, or making amends through actively and intentionally living out the values that were previously violated.

If the violation was caused by others, particularly if they were close to you, you may disengage from them with the intent of punishing them for their behavior. Sometimes people even disconnect from the whole group or community if one or more community members violated their values. They may want to punish the group, perhaps holding anger, disgust, and contempt for its members. Although these emotions are understandable, holding onto them can take a toll on you while having little to no impact on those you mean to punish. *You* end up suffering inside of the anger, rather than causing the individuals you're angry with to suffer.

Let's consider Henry's story from chapter 1. If Henry is angry and disgusted at the leadership that ordered him to capture the insurgent, these feelings might be well justified. However, if he nurses the anger and disgust, if he doesn't let these feelings rise and fall, but instead fosters them, dwelling on how they wronged him for ordering him to take the action he took, he can get stuck. His hope for their punishment backfires. *He* is suffering from his own anger and disgust. He may be less able to engage his values, and his anger may spread onto those who are close to him at home, causing further struggle.

Rigidity About Values

People who feel disconnected from their values after experiencing a violation often develop rigidity around those values, especially concerning violations committed by others. Values are meant to be approached flexibly. In life's journey, you may not always be able to move in a straight line. Insisting on a perfectly straight path may place you right in front of insurmountable obstacles; being willing to reroute allows you to keep progressing. In the same way, insisting that others adhere to your values at all times and in highly specific ways may actually block your path as well.

Remember Ellen from chapter 1? She was sexually assaulted by her schoolmates and then disregarded by her counselor and parents. Imagine that she deeply valued trust and compassion. These values were violated not only by her peers but also by her mentor and her loved ones. If, as a result, Ellen were to rigidly hold her values of trust and compassion, she might experience renewed pain whenever she or others were not entirely trusting and compassionate. She may begin to avoid all relationships, fearful that others are not fully trustworthy, compassionate, or both. She may struggle in her current relationships by setting standards for trust and compassion that others cannot meet. Her rigidity would likely make it harder for her to engage meaningfully with other people.

Exercise 6.3: Engaging with Your Previously Violated Values

Now that we've briefly described some of the ways that people can get disconnected from their values after experiencing a values violation, we invite you to explore your own relationship with your violated values. Before you begin, return to Exercise 6.1 to note here the value(s) violated:

_____

Now read the following questions and write your answers on the lines provided.

1. Is the value that was violated still vital to you in some way? Notice how it still has meaning for you.

_____

_____

_____

2. Where did you learn this value? What group or community did it come from (for example, family, school, faith community)?

_____

_____

3. Do you continue to seek out opportunities to engage in this value? If so, how? If not, what sorts of thoughts, feelings, or barriers seem to get in the way? Hint: Consider the previous descriptions of how people become disconnected from their values.

_____

_____

_____

_____

_____

4. How would you like to engage with this value going forward? Give some specific examples of actions you would like to take—big or small—that would be consistent with this value. For example, if you have been staying away from people you care about, you might consider how you could spend time with those individuals.

_____

_____

_____

_____

_____

_____

_____

It *is* possible to live your values going forward. Indeed, the very pain that you feel as a result of the values violation likely comes from your values compass strongly orienting you toward what matters. In the next section, we will explore how our pain often tells us what is important to us.

Values and Pain: Two Sides of the Same Coin

You've heard the expression "two sides of the same coin." It's generally applied to two opposing aspects of a single situation or experience. Moral injury offers a perfect example. On one side is your values; on the other is your pain. There is almost no space between them. They cannot be separated. They are two sides of the same experience.

If you did not experience pain following the values violation, it is unlikely that whatever happened in that event mattered to you. No pain = no sense of caring. We feel pain because we care. Let's examine your moral injury coins, and then consider together what to do with them.

Exercise 6.4: Your Coins, and What to Do with Them

Take a moment to consider the violated values you marked in Exercise 6.1. Notice the pain that is present when you consider what happened and how your values were violated. For example, you may notice that you value honesty and integrity, and you experience anger and disgust at having been betrayed. Maybe you value honoring God's will, and you experience shame and self-doubt because of your actions. Now, take a look at *your* experience of pain.

On one side of one or more of the coins in the figure, name your pain (for example, shame or unworthiness). You can use any word or words that you'd like to describe the hurtful moral judgments and emotions with which you struggle. (If you need more coins for this exercise, you can draw as many as you need on a separate sheet.)

Next, explore which values are on the flip side of this pain. Refer back to the list of values in Exercise 6.1, if you need to. The first coin is filled out as an example with the value (integrity) on one side and the pain at having violated that value (shame) on the other.

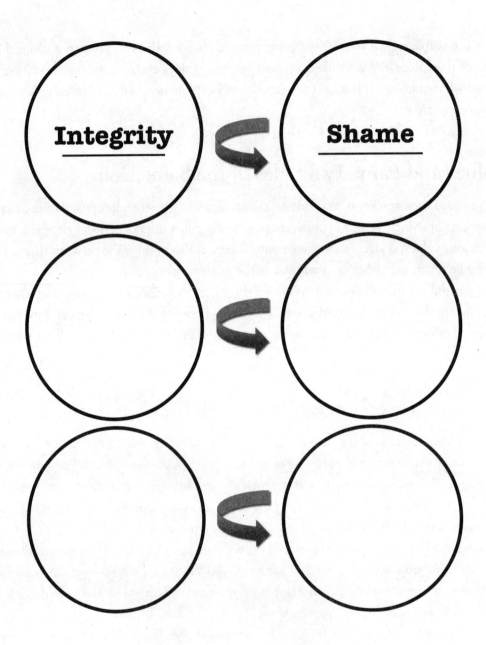

As you look at the coins, consider whether your pain might be an important signal: a reminder of your values, and maybe a call to action. Now consider something crucially important to how you will proceed from here. In noticing that your pain and your values are inextricably linked, would you still work to avoid or eliminate the pain? If eliminating the pain *also* means eliminating the value(s), how will you proceed? Trying to throw out only one side of the coin doesn't work. If you are not willing to feel the pain, you also cut yourself off from your value(s). Take a moment to reflect on this issue, then describe your thoughts here.

_____

_____

_____

_____

It is essential to become aware of both sides of your coins. We understand that you are deeply aware of the pain; now we invite you to become deeply aware of the values that are there, just millimeters away, on the other side of that coin.

Values and Moral Injury

Recall that moral values are social values, and these are often among the values violated in morally injurious experiences. Disconnection from values resulting from moral injury not only means disconnection from what is meaningful to you personally; it also means detachment from the values that connect you to the people around you.

If you reflect on the examples in the stories we have shared, you can see how each person suffered in relationship to another person or persons. For them, and likely for you, stepping back onto the values path likely means stepping back into that social community—reconnecting with others in values-aligned ways.

Moral Healing Is Reconnecting with Values

If moral pain is the outcome of violated moral values, and moral injury is the outcome of ongoing disconnection from these values, then perhaps it makes sense that moral healing is about reconnecting with values. Your moral compass is not broken. Instead, it is clearly pointing you down a path. The pain is telling you this. However, it may be that the values-based path in front of you, although meaning-filled and life-enriching, will take you through difficult terrain that will be both challenging and painful. You may question whether the journey is worth it. You may doubt your ability to make the trip. Indeed, you may even be thinking that you can't reenter the path until the pain is gone. However, stepping back onto the path *even with* the pain is the way to moral healing.

Exercise 6.5: Values Bull's-eyes

In this exercise, we invite you to do two things. First, you will identify several values that you hold in different contexts or communities in your life. Second, you'll identify how closely you are aligned with these values, as indicated by your actions. To do this, use the values bull's-eyes provided here and follow the numbered steps.

1. First, choose four contexts, communities, or roles that you want to explore in this exercise. Examples might include work, faith community, parent, friend, or partner. Write each of the four on one of the lines above the blank bull's-eyes, as shown in the completed example.

2. Next, label each of the four quadrants of the bull's-eye with a value you have in that context, community, or role.

3. Last, place an X in each quadrant of the bull's-eye according to where you think your actions fall currently in terms of lining up with that value. The more in line they are with the value, the closer to the center you will place the mark. Mark how aligned your actions are *now,* in your current day-to-day life, not where they were in the distant past.

Example:

Look at each section of your completed bull's-eyes and notice which X's are near the center and which are not. Where the mark is far from the center, reflect on what is keeping you from getting closer to the center. Right now, all you need to do is notice where you seem to be "off center." Save these bull's-eyes. We will return to values-based living through committed action in chapter 11.

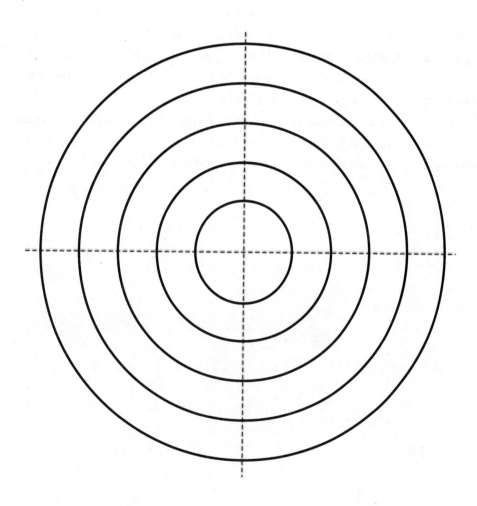

Moral healing is all about reconnecting with values. As you journey back in the direction your moral compass points to, it's essential that you clarify your values and recognize that the pain is not interfering with, but is connected to, those values. Making and keeping commitments in line with those values (chapter 11) will aid you on your journey.

Summary

Pain and values are two sides of the same coin. After a moral violation, it is important to clarify and recognize your relationship with your values. Reconnecting socially and working to keep your actions aligned with your values compass can lead to tremendous healing. (For extra practice read and complete the worksheet Values as the Flip Side of Moral Pain downloadable at http://www.newharbinger.com/44772.)

All of us, as we move forward, hope to grow the capacity to accept what is past, to be willing to have whatever is here and now, and to look to future possibilities. In chapter 7, we focus on acceptance and how it, too, can help you to live your values.

Accepting Moral Pain in the Service of Vital Living

We delight in the beauty of the butterfly, but rarely admit the changes it has gone through to achieve that beauty.

—Maya Angelou

In chapter 6, we explored your values, focusing on clarifying and reconnecting to what is most important to you. Values clarification is an essential part of healing from moral injury, but it doesn't stand alone. Healing involves a sustained effort that includes mindful awareness, connecting to a sense of self that is larger than experience, and a willingness to feel, sense, and think what is there to be felt, sensed, and thought. We'll be building this last portion—willingness, or acceptance—in this chapter. To heal, you need to engage this openness as an alternative to avoidance and control. Let's explore.

What Is Acceptance?

In chapter 2, we shared the observation of Wilson and DuFrene (2008) that people and their emotions are like sunsets, not like math problems. We are here to experience emotions, not control them. This may be different from what you have learned. From early childhood most of us are taught to fix, control, or eliminate our uncomfortable emotions. We are told that emotions are much like math problems—that is, unpleasant emotions are a problem to be figured out and solved. We've learned that we must work to change or get rid of uncomfortable emotions in order to feel happy, relieved, or at peace. But what if what we have learned is wrong?

We can control many things in our lives. For instance, we can build buildings, making safe places for us to live. We can grow crops, ensuring that we have food. We can even manipulate ones and zeros to form a computer language. It is impressive what we are able to control.

But notice where these examples of effective control occur. Effective control happens *outside* of us. We are very good at controlling our environment and manipulating it to make great advances for humankind. However, if we take those same efforts and apply them to the stuff *inside* of us—emotions, thoughts, and sensations—something very different happens. The more we try to fix, problem solve, manage, or avoid our emotions, the stronger they become, and the more frequently they tend to occur.

The Paradox of Control Inside of Us

In chapter 2, we introduced a new and perhaps somewhat strange idea. Our suggestion was that pain, even the deep psychological pain that can give way to moral injury, is *not* the problem. Rather, it is our unworkable, costly, and damaging efforts to control or eliminate the pain that leads to suffering and even more loss. The more we try to *not* think about something, the more we end up thinking about it.

Imagine that you are trying to stop thinking about the memory of a painful event, yet it keeps surfacing, again and again. You are trying hard not to think you are unworthy, yet "unworthy" appears in your mind, over and over. Herein lies the paradox. If you do not want to think about something, you have to think about it to know that you don't want to think about it! You end up in a battle within your mind. Trying hard not to think about something actually makes it harder to stop thinking about it. It's a battle that can't be won.

Exercise 7.1: Don't Think About a Gorilla

A classic ACT exercise to demonstrate the paradox of control involves trying to not think about something. Set a timer so that an alarm will ring in one minute. During that time, try to not think about a gorilla. When you start the timer, do whatever it takes to not think about any kind of gorilla. When the alarm goes off, consider how you did. Write about your experience here:

_____

_____

_____

_____

You likely found it difficult to not think about a gorilla. Perhaps the word "gorilla" popped into your mind every few seconds or so. Or perhaps you found yourself seeing images of gorillas. Interesting, isn't it? You probably don't have gorillas in your life in some ongoing way. Typically, gorillas may not enter your mind much at all. Yet you find yourself thinking about them more when you are asked to *not* think about them.

Some of you may have successfully avoided thinking about gorillas for most of the minute. But also notice how much of that minute you spent actively thinking about other things *specifically* to avoid thinking about gorillas. Even in this case, your efforts to avoid thinking about gorillas controlled and limited what you could think about.

Now, imagine how much more difficult it would be to try to not think about your morally injurious event—something that actually is a part of your life and has meaning for you. Also, notice the time, energy, and opportunities lost to the effort you expend trying to avoid thinking about those experiences.

This paradox happens not only with thinking; it happens with emotion as well. If it is really important for you to not experience an emotion, it is quite likely you are already experiencing it.

Why would it be important to not feel something? It is important only if feeling it becomes a burden in your life and can be so only if you are already feeling it. Sometimes we try so hard to *not* feel certain feelings that we end up feeling *more* of them. You may have anxiety about your anxiety, or sadness that you feel sad. You may feel guilty about your guilt or disgusted over your feelings of disgust. See how it works? When it seems really important to fix, eliminate, solve, or control an emotion, we end up feeling even more of that emotion.

The more you try to control your moral pain, the more it lingers or even intensifies. You may have heard the old saying, "What you resist, persists." This is true for emotional experience and for moral pain.

Exercise 7.2: Tug-of-War

In this imaginary game of tug-of-war (Hayes et al., 2012), you'll simulate the struggle you may be experiencing with trying to control your emotions.

1. Close your eyes for a moment and come into contact with an emotional experience connected to the moral injury that you find most difficult. Locate this experience in your body.

2. Now imagine that you could pull this emotional experience outside of you, set it in front of you, and give it a living, breathing shape. What would this emotional experience look like if you could bring it to life? Describe it:

    _____

    _____

    _____

3. Now imagine that this shape is facing you, across from a very deep hole, so deep and dark that you can't see the bottom. Imagine that this shape is holding one end of a rope, you are holding the other end, and you are each pulling the rope tight over the deep hole in a full-on game of tug-of-war with this emotional "monster." Answer the following questions:

    a. How long have you been in this tug-of-war with your moral pain?

        _____

    b. What do you miss out on or give up as a result of being in this tug-of-war? Notice where your focus is and how tied up your hands and feet are in the effort to try to pull the "monster" toward you and down into the hole. Describe what you notice:

        _____

        _____

c. As you tug, see if you can introduce some flexibility. What else might you be able to do instead of being stuck in this game?

_____

_____

d. What if you were to drop the rope? Write about what it would mean to stop playing tug-of-war—to simply drop the rope:

_____

_____

_____

_____

e. Notice that dropping the rope doesn't make the moral injury monster go away. The emotional pain is still there. However, when you are no longer trying to win the game, to control the emotion by overcoming it, you are free to move about in your life. Your hands and feet are now available for other activities, like values-based actions. Write about what you might do and where you might go now that you are no longer holding the rope and engaging with the monster:

_____

_____

_____

_____

_____

You can let go of the struggle to try to control the experience of pain. Trying to control it only sustains it or makes it more difficult, anyway. Remember, your emotions are not like math problems, to be solved and eliminated. They are like sunsets, to be observed and experienced.

"Dropping the rope" doesn't make the monster go away. Your pain remains part of your experience. And at certain times, the monster might try to reengage you in another round of tug-of-war. Dropping the rope is an ongoing process. Acceptance is an ongoing process that requires awareness and willingness in each moment. Let's continue exploring acceptance as the alternative to control.

Acceptance as the Alternative to Control

If there is no way to "fix" or control your moral pain, then what do you do? What is the alternative to control? Acceptance, or a complete willingness to feel and think whatever you feel and think. Acceptance is part of the pathway to moral healing.

Right now you may have doubts; perhaps you have tried a version of acceptance before. But we ask for your patience yet again. Willingness to experience is a muscle to be built and a process to be continually engaged. It involves openness and choice. Willingness is a path back to living your values, even—perhaps especially—those values that were previously violated. As well, willingness is an active and conscious process. It is about releasing yourself into full acceptance while being present to the ongoing flow of internal experience and then choosing the values-based action you want to engage in.

Acceptance is *not* about concession. Acceptance doesn't mean that what happened is okay. Rather, acceptance acknowledges that the past cannot be undone. History moves in only one direction. Therefore, the past will always be there—there are no do-overs. Willingness is about acknowledging the past as well as the pain that is still present and, from this place of acceptance, turning toward a future defined by your values. Struggling with a past action or event that cannot be changed only adds to suffering by continuing a life defined by pain rather than by values.

Further, being accepting doesn't mean that you want the moral pain or that you must like it. You don't have to want or like moral pain in order to accept it. Acceptance is a stance you're taking. It is about openness to experience, pleasant or unpleasant, and a full and open willingness to let it rise and fall.

Let's try an exercise to demonstrate the distinction between acceptance and control.

Exercise 7.3: Holding a Pen

1. Holding a pen (or pencil) in each hand, sit in a chair with your elbows at your sides and your hands in front of you, palms facing upward and a pen resting in each hand.

2. Allow the pen in one hand to rest gently in your open palm.

3. With the other hand, begin to squeeze the other pen as tightly as you can, as if the pen were actually quite powerful and you had to hold on tightly to keep it from moving. Without hurting yourself, bear down on the second pen with all the strength of your fingers, hand, and arm. Continue squeezing the pen, noticing the physical sensations and urges that you feel as you squeeze.

You might notice the initial tension of squeezing, which then gives way to a tingling sensation and a growing numbness in your gripping hand (don't let up—keep squeezing!).

4. Compare these sensations with the sensations you notice in your open hand—the one where the other pen is simply resting. In what ways do they feel different from one another? Where is your attention naturally pulled? But don't stop! Keep squeezing the pen.

   At this point, your clenched fist is probably feeling tired and starting to ache, and you may be ready to stop squeezing. But we aren't finished quite yet.

5. Squeeze hard for a few more seconds.

6. Now stop squeezing and open that hand slowly. As you do so, pay close attention to the sensations. Slowly open...notice the sensations...continue slowly opening, and continue noticing. You might find that after squeezing so hard, for so long, your closed fist actually is hard to open—like it's resisting opening up. Your hand will have impressions and indentations where the pen was pressed into it.

7. What else do you notice? Take a few moments to write about your observations. Compare and contrast letting the pen rest in one hand and squeezing the pen in the other.

_____

_____

_____

_____

_____

We hope this exercise is giving you a good sense of the difference between acceptance (the open palm) and control (the tightly squeezed hand). Acceptance involves a quality of openness. The way your open hand felt, simply letting the pen rest there? That's the feeling. Acceptance, in the case of moral pain, has the quality of a gentle resting of the emotion inside you—even if the emotion is difficult. Remember, no emotion or thought has the capacity to harm you. Only behavior can lead to those kinds of problems.

Let's engage in one last task for this exercise. Imagine that a difficult emotion or thought related to your moral injury could rest inside you in the same way the pen rested in the palm of your open hand. What if you didn't have to squeeze against it? What if you could fully accept it? (Notice whether anything about this seems difficult—for instance, your mind saying *It can't be done.*) Write your response:

_____

_____

_____

_____

Acceptance may mean *greater* contact with the painful emotion. But would you be willing to feel it if that enabled you to live your values again? Realize, too, that when we engage control rather than acceptance, we close ourselves off to other things, wasting a huge amount of energy and causing more damage in the process (like the indentations in your hand from the pen).

Let's continue to explore the differences between openness or willingness and being closed off or unwilling.

When the Mind and Heart Aren't Open

As we consider the roles of mind and heart in acceptance, you might be able to get a sense of where acceptance is slightly easier. People tend to be more forgiving when it comes to issues of the heart. A kind of softening can happen when you think about emotional pain and its felt qualities. Have you ever seen someone lay their hand on their own chest in the area of their heart when they are in pain? This seems to be a kind of "holding": a recognition that something is hard, and an offer of compassion by placing the hand over the heart. By the way, you can make this gesture even when that recognition and compassion seem impossible. We invite you to try it when you are feeling the pain of the moral injury.

Acceptance of what goes on in the mind is more challenging. This is partly because it is so easy to get caught up in what the mind is thinking about. We quite easily get lost in thought. In fact, we can become so lost that we forget that, although we *have* a mind, we are actually much *more* than our mind (as explored in chapter 4). Mindfulness is always useful here. Practicing "seeing" thoughts can help us to get just enough of a separation from the mind that we are no longer a slave to it.

Acceptance of painful thoughts is also challenging because we've gotten a strong, repeated message that we should be able to control what goes on in our mind. So we not only get stuck in our thoughts but also feel bad that we can't control them. This is a recipe for nonacceptance!

Have you ever told your mind to simply "let go" of whatever it is dwelling on, but it didn't obey? Have you ever told your mind to just forget about that persistent thought, and it didn't listen? Remember, as we explored earlier in this chapter, trying to not think about something keeps that very thing in your mind. The mind doesn't obey or listen, especially if you are asking it to obey or forget a particularly powerful and painful event.

So we've titled this section "When the mind and heart aren't open." What happens when you are unwilling to think and feel what you think and feel? This is something for you to notice on your own. What happens to you when your mind and heart are not open? Most readers struggling with moral injury will say that they feel disconnected, perhaps alone in their struggle. You might say that nothing seems the same anymore; life has changed, and not for the better. Your relationship with yourself may be harsh and unforgiving. You might carry resentment of others. You might feel cut off and isolated.

Nonacceptance: Moral Pain versus Moral Injury

One other thing happens when mind and heart are not open. Unworkable control efforts turn natural (albeit uncomfortable) moral pain into the lived suffering of moral injury. Working to not feel the moral pain and to not remember the event often requires strategies that end up further violating personally held values. Perhaps it is the control efforts themselves that lead to the great suffering that follows a morally injurious event. A terrible thing happened, and then more terrible things continue to happen as we battle with the emotions and thoughts that emerged from the event.

The Outcome of Acceptance of Moral Pain: Vital Living

Accepting moral pain allows you to once more embrace the values on the flip side of that pain. Willingness to think and feel what you think and feel allows you to step out of the control battle and back into your life. Here you can focus on creating meaning and living with vitality—even if your mind says you do not deserve to. In this reengagement, you stop violating the values that were originally breached. You again open yourself to life and all of its ups and downs, its deep pain and amazing joy. Willingness to have moral pain also allows you to receive and *learn* from the important social signals (such as guilt signaling need for restitution).

Acceptance in the Context of Our Social Worlds

Morally injurious events bring into sharp focus the flaws and imperfections of human beings. We hurt one another. We let ourselves and each other down, sometimes in dramatic and terrible ways. Depending on the nature of the morally injurious event, this can include witnessing how other humans can at times be self-interested and callused to the needs of others. For others, the morally injurious event or perhaps their ways of coping afterward may bring into focus how at times we also can lack compassion and stray from our own values.

Acceptance in the face of moral injury means, in part, continuing to engage with humanity. But how can we when we are confronted with imperfections from the past, the present, and the foreseeable future? Many of the exercises identified in this and the preceding chapters highlight how, when we step back from our own experience, we often come to realize that things are not always as they seem. In chapter 4, we learned that our self-perceptions can actually obscure a sense of ourselves that is bigger, deeper, and more resilient than any mind-constructed identity. In chapter 5, we learned that rigidly following moral rules can actually hinder us from living our values; in chapter 6, we learned that values and moral pain are actually two sides of the same coin. In this chapter, we've learned that pushing experiences away can actually make them stick around longer. None of these new insights are intuitive; in fact, they are often the opposite of what we might expect.

Human imperfection provides yet another paradox that can aid you in your process of moral healing. By accepting that we and others around us at the present moment live our values imperfectly, we free ourselves to engage with our values *more* perfectly. Values themselves are always perfect. Fairness, justice, integrity, honor, loyalty, and compassion are all ideals that we fall short of when we compare ourselves or others to them. When we notice this discrepancy, our internal compass is activated and we feel moral pain. ACT teaches that this crucial moment, when we are in pain, makes all the difference. If, on one hand, we reject the pain and in so doing reject ourselves or others with it, we reject our connection to values and to humanity itself. If, on the other hand, we continue to keep heart and mind open to that pain, to learn and be guided by it, it can draw us into deeper, more fulfilling relationships with our values, ourselves, and those around us.

Summary

Engaging from a stance of acceptance of our past, our thoughts, and our emotions allows us to step forward. If we are no longer engaged in unworkable efforts to not think and feel what we think and feel, we free ourselves to take steps that move us in new directions. As noted in chapter 6, we are hopeful that this new freedom can enable actions in line with your personal values. Being open, aware, and engaged is the antidote to suffering, both at a personal level and in relationship to your community. The place to live your values is here and the time to live them is now. (For extra practice read and complete the worksheet Embracing Moral Pain in the Service of Vital Living downloadable at http://www.newharbinger .com/44772.)

We turn next, in chapter 8, to living in the moment. Bringing your heart and mind along, remain open and accepting in your efforts to step back onto the path of values.

Living Your Values in the Present Moment

There are only two days in the year that nothing can be done. One is called yesterday and the other is called tomorrow. Today is the right day to love, believe, do and mostly live.

—The Dalai Lama

We have just explored the paradox of trying to control our thoughts, emotions, and sensations. We observed how trying to push these internal experiences away can actually lead to more difficulties. When you are fighting to control your pain, you have the pain plus the fight. Suffering is the result. The alternative is willingness to experience, or opening up to your thoughts, emotions, and sensations. Becoming aware of your experience in the moment, in the here and now, observing the flow of experience as it rises and falls: this is part of the work of acceptance. In this chapter, we explore living well in the present moment.

The Importance of the Present Moment

Living with moral injury often means being captured by your past. The injury occurred in history and lingers into the present. This is not surprising. Minds have an incredible capacity to remember; indeed, it is part of their job to do just that. Minds do not remember everything, but they are generally designed to remember painful or difficult events. Remembering these events serves as a kind of safety mechanism, a protection or forewarning, to avoid painful or traumatic events in the future.

More problematically, without our consent or desire, minds can take us back to the event again and again, reminding us of our struggle, despite any desire to forget or overcome. Our experience of this type of remembering is often intrusive and especially bothersome to those who experience uninvited thoughts. You are not alone in being captured by your past—by your moral injury. It happens to everyone to different degrees.

Some people become so captured by their past that they find themselves dwelling on it far more than expected, and in unanticipated situations. Their current life experience becomes filled with the memories, sensations, and other experiences linked to the morally injurious event. For some, their life becomes so captured by what happened that a considerable amount of what is going on here and now becomes connected to what happened back then. Those suffering with moral injury may worry that they will never enjoy life more fully again compounding the struggle. Captured by their past and worrying about their future, they can end up in a difficult psychological and emotional place. In this struggle, they may feel unable to forgive themselves or others. They think about themselves in often harsh and critical ways. Their current experience becomes tainted by this criticism.

These criticisms can also bleed into their futures in a relentless stream of thoughts: they'll forever deserve punishment; justice will never be served, fairness never delivered; recovery is simply not possible. These experiences lead to a never-ending sense of suffering. The future seems hopeless, bleak, and without vitality.

Let's take a look at how this plays out even in just a single day.

Exercise 8.1: Missing the Now

In this exercise you will explore how much time your mind spends "outside" of the now. Consider each question, then mark on the line how much time you spend in the past and in the future. It's hard to know for sure, so take your best guess at the amount of time.

1. How much time in a single, sixteen-hour day (minus the typical eight hours of sleep) do you spend dwelling on the *past*? Take time to reflect and consider all the different situations and ways in which your mind might be dwelling on something that happened in the past: for instance, thinking about what happened in the last week, the day before today, or even the past hour. Mark an X to indicate the approximate amount of time:

0 hours   8 hours   16 hours
- -

2. How much time in a single sixteen-hour day do you spend thinking about the *future?* This includes worry, planning, daydreaming, and so on. Take time to reflect and consider all the different situations and ways in which your mind might be spending time on what is to come. Mark an X to indicate the approximate amount of time:

0 hours   8 hours   16 hours
- -

3. Take time to reflect on the amount of time you indicated for each, past and future. Combined, how much time in a single sixteen-hour day do you spend thinking about what *was* or what *will be?*

0 hours   8 hours   16 hours
- -

Notice how much time in a week, month, and year you devote to what is past and what hasn't happened yet. Doing the math will show how little time you spend in the here and now. Reflect on the lost moments—moments lost in the struggle against what was or what will be. Each taking away from what is. Each moving you away from where life happens—the here and now.

Vitality Occurs in the Moment

Vitality occurs only in the here and now, in this moment. Our capacity to remember the past and think about the future deceives us. It makes it seem as if the past and future are where life happens. Your mind's ability to revisit what has already happened, although useful at times (like when recalling the directions to work or home) or pleasant for many reasons (like when reflecting on a special moment), takes you away from what is happening in the now. You lose the connection to the immediate, felt sense of the moment. This can take you away—and into suffering.

Let's look at how this can happen by exploring an example. Maggie was forced by circumstance to make a decision that resulted in great moral distress. Over time, her attempts to make this pain go away led to the additional suffering we call moral injury.

Maggie was a single mom, pregnant with fraternal twins. When they were born, one child suffered from severe birth defects that left only a tiny chance of short-term survival and no prospect of life quality. Experimental interventions were likely to be painful and unlikely to meaningfully extend life. Hospital staff suggested the possibility of palliative care to allow the infant to die naturally and free from pain. This was Maggie's choice.

The years of anguish following this decision were filled with guilt and self-criticism. Had she made the right choice? Had she done the right thing? Caring for the twin who survived reminded her of this choice daily. In her mind, she would return to those moments in the hospital, recalling and reflecting on her choice over and over again.

Maggie also worried about the future. Would others find out? Would she be viewed with disdain and disgust if others learned of her decision? Would she always be unhappy, unable to forgive herself? Maggie spends hours thinking about what had happened and about what could have been.

The full cost of this consuming process also goes beyond Maggie. Maggie's suffering has made her not fully available to her surviving child. She has lost moment after moment with her living child, giving them over to her painful thoughts about the infant who had passed. Maggie's grief and guilt are consuming her life.

Not only is Maggie suffering by being captured by her past and future, she is also missing what is happening in her present life. Maggie has another child to love and care for. Her guilt and grief about her past choices humanize her and inform her about what she values— a deep caring and love of children. However, Maggie's self-criticism about her past and her constant fight to try and make the pain go away leave her stuck in her history. In her efforts to control her internal experience, Maggie is transported across time and space—living within what happened instead of living for what *is*.

She is missing precious moments filled with opportunity to engage her values in the present—to take part in deep caring with and for her living child. She is missing opportunities to create new, enduring memories of happiness shared between them.

Living with *vitality* is an experience of energy, significance, passion, and animation. Vital moments throughout our lives, both painful and joyful, help us to identify what is most important and meaningful. Missing these moments means missing out on meaningful living. Life becomes about the past rather than the only true place where life occurs—the here and now.

The next exercise will help you take a closer look at the vitality in your life.

Exercise 8.2: Noticing the Most Vital Places in Your Life

In this exercise, you will reflect on two memories and then write about your experience.

1. Sit comfortably where you won't be disturbed. Close your eyes and bring to mind a difficult memory from your life that is *not* about the morally injurious event. Perhaps it is a loss or disappointment, an argument in a relationship, or a time when things didn't go as planned. Now take time to wander around in this memory. Notice the sights and sounds of the memory and all that was happening. Notice who you were with, if anyone, and what their presence brought to the experience. After spending several moments with the memory, take a minute to reflect on any part of it that felt vital or significant. Write about what you discovered:

_____

_____

_____

_____

2. Now close your eyes and bring to mind a pleasant memory from your life. Perhaps it is a time when you felt loved or connected, a special time like a birthday or anniversary, or a time when things worked out just right. Take time to wander around in this memory. Notice the sights and sounds of the memory and all that was happening. Notice who you were with, if anyone, and what their presence brought to the experience. After spending some time with the memory, take a minute to reflect on any part of it that felt vital or important. Write about what you discovered:

_____

_____

_____

_____

3.   Now take time to consider both memories. Notice whether the vitality of each experi-
     ence wasn't in your reflections about the past or future. See if the vitality was happening
     in the moment that the memory was being created. Notice if the vitality was in what you
     actually heard, sensed, felt, saw, and experienced in these important times. Notice any
     impact that the people with you made on the vitality of the experience. Notice how the
     importance of the experience can diminish if you are not in the moment—how it can be
     consumed by what could have been. Vitality arrives when you live your life in the moment.

Connecting to the moment and living more fully there are a part of creating our personal meaning across time. Living your values in the moment—being present to what you
sense, think, and feel, as well as being present with those you love—is vitality.

Heart and Mind

We hope that in Exercise 8.2 you were able to get a sense of how those critical or powerful
moments created meaning for you. When we look back on the times that were most important to us, the ones that reflect our personal meaning, those are often the times when we
were more fully connected to someone or something important in that moment. We were
fully present to what was happening—feeling, sensing, and connecting to the here and now.

That said, recognizing this does not take away our past. The moral emotions of the
heart, the pain that you feel about what happened—these will rise and fall. Allowing these
experiences to come and go will be a part of living in the moment. Living outside of the
moment is about getting enveloped by the emotion, no longer observing its rise and fall, but
instead getting captured by it. When this happens, the mind is likely involved. The emotion
rises as it is triggered. In Maggie's case, it might happen while planning an outing with her
child and suddenly remembering that she has only one of her twins. She might then fall into
the memory of the past, being captured by her mind and dwelling on the morally injurious
event and its fallout, her mind criticizing her and pulling her away from the moment. Now,
there may well be a time to reflect on the moral injury—this makes sense to us. Remembering
the event is inevitable. However, being captured by it is not. We can always make the effort
to reconnect to the present moment.

There are a number of mindfulness exercises; we recommend trying as many as you are
willing to. Some may appeal to you more than others. The main goal is to find ones that
will help you to regularly practice living in the moment through mindful awareness of what

is happening in the here and now. You'll gain the most benefit by practicing without judgment or self-criticism.

The next exercise details three mindfulness practices to help you grow your ability to live more fully in the moment. Read each one first, then give it a try, now or whenever you can. We also provide mindfulness resources in the handout for this chapter (available at http://www.newharbinger.com/44772) so you can continue to practice throughout your lifetime, living more often in the here and now—where choice and vitality lie.

Exercise 8.3: Mindfulness

Prepare for each of these by setting a timer for one to five minutes. If you have practiced mindfulness in the past, feel free to set the timer for a longer period. If you are new to mindfulness, we suggest starting with a shorter period. For all three, sit in a comfortable position with both feet squarely on the floor. Sit up with a firm but not rigid posture and start the timer.

1. Awareness of the Breath. A common mindfulness practice.

   a. Gently close your eyes or gaze softly on a spot on the floor in front of you. Bring your attention to your breath at the tip of your nose. Begin to notice the flow of your breath as it passes in and out of your nostrils. Using your attention, follow the breath all the way in and all the way out. If it helps you focus, you can say to yourself *breathing in* on the in-breath and *breathing out* on the out-breath. Simply follow your breath with focused attention. If your attention gets drawn away to other places, or if your mind gets busy, simply acknowledge without judgment that you lost focus, return your attention to the tip of your nose, and again follow the breath as it moves in and out of your body. If you are drawn away a hundred times, acknowledge and return a hundred times. That is the *practice* of mindfulness—returning to the moment again and again. When the timer alarm sounds, take a deep slow breath, ending your practice.

   b. Do this as often possible, even daily if you choose. The more you engage in this kind of more formal practice, the more you will be able to stay present.

2. Awareness of the Senses. In this exercise, you will focus your attention on a particular sense for a period of time. You can set a timer if you like, or simply focus your attention on each sense for a period that feels right to you. The goal is to be in the moment as often as possible.

a.   Turn your attention to your hearing. Focus on sound, noticing all the different sounds around you. If you are outside, you might notice the sounds of nature. If you are indoors, you might notice the air conditioner or furnace or voices in the background. Notice the intensity (how loud or quiet) or quality (sharp or soft) of the sound. Notice the rise and fall of sound as you continue listening. Spend a few moments (or the time you've set) on hearing before moving on to the next sense.

b.   Turn your attention to seeing. Focus on what you see. You can notice many different colors and objects, or you can place your attention on a single object like a tree or flower. Let yourself gently focus on seeing, attending to both the smaller details and the bigger picture of what you see. Spend a few moments on seeing before moving on to the next sense.

c.   Finally, turn your attention to touch. Focus on the sensations that you experience on your skin. For instance, the breeze on your cheek if you are outside, or the feel of the rough or smooth upholstery or wood of your chair against your hands. Feel the texture of objects as you hold or touch them. Spend a few moments on feeling before moving on.

d.   Practice shifting your focus among the senses. For instance, if you are outside, you might first attend to what you hear for a period, and then to what you see, and finally to sensations on your skin. Gently move to different senses as you practice focusing on your senses in each new moment.

3.   Awareness of Pace: Moving slowly—physically changing the speed at which you take certain actions—can change your awareness and increase the level of conscious behavioral control and the intentionality of your movements. This provides greater control over behavior so you can bring it more in line with your chosen values. Here's one way to get a sense of this.

a.   Write your signature as many times as you can for sixty seconds on the lines provided (if you think you will need more space, use a separate piece of paper).

_____

_____

_____

_____

_____

b. Afterward, note what that experience was like (painful, boring, sloppy, mindless). Now write your signature again, but this time write in super _slow motion_ so that you write your signature just once in the entire sixty-second period. Don't worry about finishing.

_____

c. Notice how this experience was different from the first time. Compare and contrast how moving quickly often involves impulsivity and habit, while moving slowly requires focus and choice.

Additional Resources: There are many resources that can assist you in building a regular practice of mindful awareness. Phone apps like _Mindfulness Coach, Headspace,_ and _Calm_ are available in Apple's App Store for iOS devices or on Google Play for Android. You can also find mindfulness exercises on YouTube, as well as audio recordings. Again, the key to living more fully in the moment is practice. Set yourself a goal of practicing at scheduled times as well as throughout your day.

Being with Others in the Present Moment

We noted earlier that being in the present moment is not simply about living in the here and now with respect to your own experience. Connecting with the present also allows us to connect with others. To better understand this, notice that when you are out of the present moment, whether dwelling on the past or caught up in anticipating the future, it's hard to relate to others in vital and dynamic ways.

Remember the example of Maggie, shared earlier in this chapter. When Maggie would hold her surviving child, she would feel self-doubt and guilt about the other twin who had passed away. Disturbed by this pain, Maggie turned inward, wrestling with unanswerable "whys" about the past and "what-ifs" about the future. With her attention drawn away from the present, she couldn't focus on the surviving twin. In this way, second by second, and minute by minute, Maggie robbed herself of meaningful moments with her living child. Her anxiety about what others might think of her decision caused her to pull away from others and robbed her of potential supportive care from those who loved her.

As you strive to be present in the here and now in your own life, it helps to recognize that you and your fellow humans are ever changing, ever evolving. Our thoughts come and go, our emotions rise and fall. We're like dancers moving across the floor, and when two or more people share a space that allows them to feel each other's presence and intentions, they have the chance to connect in the moment. They can move together in harmony, not just physically, but also emotionally. This synergy is beautiful because, when we connect in the present moment, we can experience the world together.

However, as soon as we try to capture and contain such a moment of connection, we trade the act of dancing itself for a future memory of the dance. Or we may seek to rush the dance, trying to force changes that the relationship is not yet ready to support. What would it mean to freeze this dance in a photo or to jump ahead to the finale? Would it capture the flow and movements of the dancers? Certainly not. Relationships between humans, like dancing, can't be frozen in time without losing their essence. When we try to prevent relationships from moving forward or push them faster than they can sustain, we fall out of sync with our partners, friends, and loved ones.

The example of Maggie also shows how, when we have lost touch, we can rejoin in the dance once more. Although still deeply grieving the loss of her other child, Maggie at times would also intentionally look down at the surviving baby. Although she was barely a few weeks old, when she reached out to grasp her mother's finger or touch her face, Maggie would be filled with awe. And as she nursed the baby, she felt a deep bond growing. Maggie saw the world reflected in her child's shining eyes. Although Maggie never forgot the baby she had lost, with time she took joy in watching her twin begin to sit, then crawl, then stand and take her first steps. The dance of life kept moving.

Actively Showing Up to the Present Without Judgment

Showing up to the present is not a passive experience. As the practice exercises in this chapter demonstrate, staying in the present moment involves a deliberate choice to stay connected with what is going on in and around us. Staying connected to the present moment, and noticing when that connection is disrupted, is an active process. It means staying connected with ourselves as much as with others with whom we wish to connect.

Because our minds are adept at analyzing the past and future, we are often unaware that we have drifted away from the present moment. For example, as Maggie gazed lovingly at the face of her child, she felt a sharp pang of grief, bringing her back to the hospital and the confusion and anguish she felt at letting go of her other child. The sudden vivid entrance of this memory into Maggie's mind captured her attention so quickly and completely that she was absorbed by it for several seconds. Maggie snapped back to the present with a jolt only when the baby in her arms began to cry. As she tended to the fussing infant, Maggie's sadness was compounded by realizing that for a minute or two she had lost touch with her responsibilities to her surviving child.

Although by no means intentional, this tendency of our mind to wander (even from our loved ones) is a normal part of consciousness. Instead of berating herself, it would have been helpful for Maggie to realize that it is normal and natural to become lost in thought, especially when experiencing painful memories or intense emotion. In these moments, criticizing and judging oneself for becoming distracted only serves to deepen and extend one's disconnection from the present moment.

Maggie's example can show us how present-moment practice is helpful. Maggie was pulled out of the past by the cry of the baby in her arms. She immediately felt a pang of fresh guilt for having drifted away again and for not having paid closer attention to her child. Her mind easily found many rules about motherhood and judgments about her performance in this role. Rather than getting lost in this never-ending downward spiral, however, Maggie took several slow breaths, scanning her body and noticing where she felt her emotions. Locating the knot in her chest that was connected to her guilt, Maggie expanded her attention outward and noticed the weight of her baby in her arms and the heat of the swaddled body. By directing her attention toward her own sensory experience in the present, Maggie was better able to find and connect to her child in keeping with her value of devoted motherhood.

The example of Maggie and her children can help us see the power of the present moment for building and strengthening human relationships. Imagine those moments in the past when you have made these types of connections. So often we are trying to *do* things and *go* places with other people. What if, instead, we practiced simply *being with* ourselves and others?

Exercise 8.4: Mindful Awareness in the Social Context

Being aware of your relationships and interactions with others is part of flourishing in the here and now. This involves attending to your experience in relationship to others. Practice mindful awareness in a social context by engaging each of the following brief exercises:

1. Mindful Seeing

    a. Look at your partner's or a loved one's face. Intentionally notice each detail. What are the curves and lines? What are the colors and shapes? What color are their eyes, their lips, their skin? Take time to look into their eyes. Hold their gaze a little longer than you might normally do. Notice what you experience as you connect with them in the moment. Let yourself feel whatever you feel as you look. Be aware and mindful of your experience.

    b. You can share what you are doing with your partner before you begin, or simply do it in small moments throughout the day.

2. Noticing Emotion

    a. Intentionally observe what others are feeling or experiencing around you. Pay attention to whether their mood is light or low. Notice if they laugh and what it sounds like. Notice how their face changes with different emotional states. Notice any sounds they make that represent that state: a sigh, for instance.

    b. Tune in to what each experience brings to you in the moment, noticing how you feel in reaction to their experiences.

3. Mindful Listening

    a. Take time to pay attention to what a loved one or friend is saying. Notice the quality of their voice. Is their voice pitched high or low? Are they speaking quickly, slowly, or at a normal pace? Are they excited, sad, or confused, or can you detect some other emotion in their voice? Can you "hear" their emotion in what they are saying?

    b. What do you notice about your own experience in the moment of noticing their experience? What do you experience when you attune to another?

Continue to grow your mindful awareness of others and your experience of them. Let yourself tune in to what is happening in the here and now in your relationships. Show up. You are invited to be in the moment with those you care about and love.

The Present Moment Is Where Choice Lives

Finally, and most importantly, *choice* lives in the present moment. In each moment of awareness, we can make choices connected to our values. If you are open to your experience, connected to a larger sense of self, observing your mind rather than being caught in it, you are free. Here you can take your next step, your next action in line with what gives you meaning.

When we are captured by our past or worried about our future, we have less choice in living our values. In this "elsewhere" place, we tend to behave more impulsively, or to hide and withdraw as we struggle. Being in the present moment, however, confers advantages for living our values; chiefly, that being in the moment maximizes our power to choose because we are more aware of what is happening and can be more intentional in our behaviors.

Your personal values begin to unfold, moment after moment, into the flow of life. How long is a moment, anyway? Try to mentally time when one moment begins and when one ends. Notice how this can't be done. Time is not divided into discrete chunks on a clock; it actually flows more like rain on a river, each drop melting seamlessly together with the drop before it and the drop after it. As you live, rather than trying to catch each moment as if you were trying to separate the drops from one another, concentrate on noticing the ongoing flow of experience. Bring your awareness to this flow across time, choosing where you place your intentions and "feet" as you go—as you, with awareness, live your values.

Summary

Living in the moment is where vitality unfolds. Being present to sensation, thought, and the ongoing flow of experiences within you and between others brings every moment to life. Practicing mindful awareness builds your ability to engage, connecting you to what you are doing and allowing you the freedom to choose. (For extra practice read and complete the worksheet Living Your Values in the Present Moment downloadable at http://www.newhar binger.com/44772.)

Now that we have explored most of the processes of well-being and flexibility—self-as-context, defusion, values, acceptance, and present moment—in part 3 we turn to two important issues related to recovery from moral injury: forgiveness and compassion. We will rely on the processes already explored in this book to support your exploration of these topics.

PART 3

Moving Forward, Living Well

CHAPTER 9

Forgiveness: To Give What Came Before

He that cannot forgive…breaks the bridge over which he himself must pass…for everyone has need to be forgiven.

—George Herbert

In part 2 of this book, we explored multiple ways to engage the process of true healing from moral injury. We focused on connecting you with a sense of yourself that is more than your experiences. From this place, you can step back and observe that you *have* a mind, yet know that you are more than your mind. From here you can also be open to emotional experience, learning to accept what you feel, think, and sense. This open, aware position frees you to live more in the moment, choosing to engage your values as you proceed through life. Engaging in this work is an ongoing effort and the pathway to recovery.

Now, in part 3, we stretch into territory that is delicate, perhaps even difficult, but in many ways necessary. Two main issues—forgiveness and compassion—make up this section of the book, followed by a committed action wrap-up in chapter 11. We dedicate a chapter to each issue, exploring its challenges and benefits as additional personal steps to healing. This chapter focuses on forgiveness.

Defining Forgiveness

From the ACT perspective, action is built into recovery. Making and keeping commitments that are consistent with your values is a defining quality of a life well-lived. With this basic idea in mind, let's focus on two meanings of the word "forgive." The first comes from its Old English origin: to give away completely the desire to punish. The second meaning is our own construction: seeing "for" as the Old English "before" and drawing on the Latin *per-donare* for the "give": "to give completely, without reservation." We see the act of forgiveness as *giving* what came *before* the harm (to *fore-give*): giving back to yourself or others the type of relationship that was there before the harm—before the moral injury.

Viewing both meanings together, forgiveness is an act of giving linked to an intention—letting go of punishment. Let's take a closer look at each.

Letting Go of Punishment

Punishment involves inflicting a penalty or engaging in retribution for the violation of a rule or code. In the context of this book, it would be about punishing yourself or someone else for a moral violation. It makes sense that those suffering with moral injury view themselves or others as deserving of punishment. They feel that those responsible must pay for the offense. We recognize the reasoning behind this position. There is a logical sort of "if, then" process that follows the violation. Our minds tell us that if someone violates a moral value, that person deserves punishment. However, if we look a little closer, we can see that *punishment itself does not repair the violation.*

Quite often, a punishment that is self-directed or wished upon others instead serves to prolong the pain of the individual who suffered the moral injury, and it may also create additional suffering for others. When creating pain is the focus, correction doesn't happen, especially when the punishment takes the form of repeated, harsh condemnations that don't change behavior for the better. Indeed, punishment of this kind can inadvertently continue to violate values long after the original violation, creating an ever-lengthening chain of even more damage and suffering.

Let's take the example of Robert from chapter 1. Robert suffered a terrible loss when he looked at a text while driving and lost his son in the ensuing car accident. Robert believed that he did not deserve forgiveness; his only son had died as a result of his error. He became harshly critical toward himself, beating himself up about his "carelessness" and "stupidity." He felt extreme guilt and disgust with his behavior. He was angry with himself for not checking the seat belts and for glancing at a text. *Only a heartless person could do something like that,* he would say to himself. Robert felt he deserved to be punished, to be alone, to suffer.

When viewed in a purely logical way, Robert's self-punishment makes sense. Robert engaged in an action that led to a permanent and terrible loss. He engaged in behavior that violated his values of responsibility and caring. Therefore, being punished through self-criticism and loathing could be seen as a "proper" or "fair" response. However, as Robert became lost in his self-punishment, something else began to happen. He began to pull away from his daughter and wife. Robert began to sink into the emotions and pain of the loss. He began to believe that he did not deserve the love of his wife and daughter and that if they left, that would be a fitting punishment as well.

Robert's family cared deeply for him and could see his pain and remorse. They would try to share and engage with him, yet he would pull away, again and again, thinking he did not deserve to be part of the family he felt he had destroyed. The whole family started to suffer. The values of responsibility and caring *continued* to be violated. Robert's way forward, including treating himself as he once did—as a husband and father connected to his family through sharing and kindness—gave way to self-criticism and absorption in the belief that he deserved to be punished. Lost in his reaction to his moral pain, Robert had lost contact with the impact his self-punishment was having on others.

Giving up the desire to punish would mean, for Robert, that he could be a husband who returned to being present and connected with his wife and daughter. But holding onto the desire to punish and withholding self-forgiveness keeps alive emotions of hurt, anger, and blame that can discolor our relationships. As we dwell on the injury, we begin to feel trapped in the past. Holding onto the suffering can lead to increased sorrow, only intensifying it and keeping it alive.

Similar patterns can happen when your moral pain stems from betrayal by someone else. Remaining angry and disgusted with someone for violating values can also affect you and those you care about in significant and negative ways. But forgiveness—letting go of punishment—can lead to resilience and healing from the struggle.

Finally, there's an important question to ask, tapping the definition that began the chapter. Punishment's true purpose is to make a correction. What needs to be corrected? We propose that the correction is about returning to values-based living—as you move through each day, reengaging the morals that were violated: honoring life, showing love or that you care, and connecting authentically with others. These are values that can be dishonored when you attempt to punish yourself or others for a moral violation. But you can honor those values by putting your feet back in motion, again aligning with your values, and engaging them fully in your behavior.

Exercise 9.1: Letting Go of Punishment

Take time to reflect on how you have punished yourself for a moral violation (or spent time wishing for or ruminating about another person or persons being punished for a moral violation). Consider the times you have been angry or disgusted with yourself or someone else as a result of a moral violation. After a period of short reflection, answer the following questions:

1. How am I affected by my continuing to punish myself and/or others?

   _____

   _____

   _____

2. How are others affected by my continuing to punish myself and/or others?

   _____

   _____

   _____

3. Has the punishment led to a correction in terms of living my values, or has it made things worse?

   _____

   _____

   _____

For the next two questions, before you respond, take more time to reflect—and be honest with yourself.

4. What might my life look like if I completely let go of the desire and power to punish myself or others?

_____

_____

_____

_____

_____

5. How might it affect others I care for if I completely let go of the desire and power to punish myself or others?

_____

_____

_____

_____

_____

Fully consider making a correction by returning to your values and letting go of punishing yourself and others. Turning toward forgiveness can help you to heal.

Giving What Came Before

When we think of forgiveness, we often think of it as a shared experience wherein two parties, one who was harmed and one who did the harming, engage in a conversation or action related to asking for forgiveness. If granted, there is usually a sense of relief and a feeling that the load has been lightened—perhaps even a feeling of peace. Following the forgiveness, there is typically some time spent by the two parties, coming back together and then moving forward and on with life.

Although we see that this can be a part of forgiveness, and the emotional states of relief and peace are welcomed, keep in mind that emotional states are temporary. Because emotions rise and fall, equating forgiveness with a feeling can jeopardize the benefits of forgiveness. We suggest that forgiveness is not a feeling at all (Walser & Westrup, 2007); rather, it is an action—an activity.

Forgiveness involves the *act* of giving. It is about returning to actions or behaviors that were present in the relationship before the harm, or in this case, the moral violation. This action is true whether it is a relationship with yourself or a relationship with someone else. Behaving in a forgiving way might then mean once again acting in kind ways, engaging in thoughtful and caring interactions, and treating yourself or others in respectful ways. Forgiveness is about behaving charitably or compassionately with oneself or with another.

The feelings associated with the act of forgiveness will come and go. Sometimes you may have feelings of relief or feel that you have been forgiven; other times you may not. You may find yourself still feeling angry or disgusted. But you can always *behave* in forgiving ways. With the acceptance of internal experience, opening to what you feel while observing the rise and fall of emotions will allow you to engage in behaviors that you care about, rather than simply settling into harmful ways of being in the world. These harmful ways of being can include punishing yourself by withdrawing, engaging in self-loathing, and keeping yourself from being connected to others. If the moral violation you experienced involved betrayal, harmful actions might include being consumed by anger at others and acting on it in ways (like plotting revenge, or ruminating on the betrayal) that hurt you or keep you from living a values-based life.

The act of forgiveness is a process, meaning that it goes on for a lifetime. As a person engaging in forgiveness, you are continuously working to behave in a manner that is about giving back what came before the harm, reengaging values that were once prioritized and were then violated in the morally injurious event. At times you will get captured by your thoughts and feelings, forgetting that you are working on forgiveness. When this happens, it is essential to acknowledge that you got caught, and to then return to giving to yourself or others the caring that came before the harm.

One reason we focus on this definition is that it explicitly frees you from relying on an emotional experience as a marker of forgiveness. Have you ever had someone slight or harm you in some way, and you forgave them? You may briefly feel better, until you think about the slight or harm again. Suddenly the memory of the slight or harm brings back the upset and anger you felt just after the harm. What happens to the forgiveness then? Relying on feeling good as a marker for forgiveness is shaky; it places actual forgiveness at risk.

Feelings rise and fall, come and go, leave and return. Thus, if you forgive yourself or someone else and base it on how you feel, you will be stuck on a forgiveness roller coaster, sometimes feeling like you have forgiven yourself or another, sometimes not. This kind of roller-coaster ride can add to your suffering. It can be confusing and make you wonder whether you have done the work of forgiveness or not. You may question the intent and outcome of the forgiveness, which leads you to doubt whether forgiveness happens at all.

We believe that forgiveness can happen as an engaged activity. But we want to separate it from the feeling of relief or lightness and instead ground it in action. We recognize that there may be other things you were dealing with before the moral injury that may lead you to be unkind to yourself, but we ask you to step outside of that experience and imagine how you might treat yourself or another if the injury or injuries you are working with had never happened.

Forgiveness Does Not Mean Forgetting

We have all heard the saying, "Forgive and forget," yet we must fully recognize that memories about moral injury are often too vivid and etched in our minds to ever be *forgotten*. In these cases, forgetting is an impossible task. So what we invite you to consider in this chapter isn't about forgetting.

The memories are so difficult that they can't be erased, but that doesn't mean we have to fight them. Instead of trying to forget the memories of moral injury, we can acknowledge when they arrive and allow them to pass. Over and over again, let them rise and fall, and then choose to turn to values-based actions. At first, this may sound like torture, but the torture isn't in the memory itself, which is there to remind you of what is important. Rather, torture comes from dwelling on the memory and punishing yourself or others when it resurfaces. Engaging with the memory in this way makes your suffering grow. Forgiveness does not erase the memory, but it is the antidote to the suffering created by struggling against it.

The words of Nelson Mandala (as portrayed by actor Morgan Freeman in the 2009 film *Invictus*) speak to the power of forgiveness: "Forgiveness starts here…. Forgiveness liberates the soul. It removes fear, That is why it is such a powerful weapon…. The past is the past; we look to the future." From our perspective, the future can be created in each present moment of values-based living, creating meaning as you step forward in your life.

Exercise 9.2: You and Giving What Came Before

1. Take a few minutes to reflect on how you had treated yourself and others before the moral injury occurred. Notice if you were in any way kinder to yourself (or to others). Perhaps you were less critical or felt that you at least deserved to be a part of life, giving and receiving what others give and receive (relationships, participation). Write what you discovered:

    _____

    _____

    _____

    _____

2. Now consider the possibility that you could begin to treat yourself that way once again. What shows up for you when you think about this? What might get in the way? Jot down a couple of barriers:

    _____

    _____

If you notice that any of the barriers are feelings (guilt, anger, sadness, disgust), thoughts (*I deserve to suffer, I could never forgive myself, people are evil*) or sensations (fast heart rate, heaviness in the chest), remember that you can mindfully observe these experiences, acknowledge how they serve you, and make a choice to give yourself or others what went before.

Forgiveness and Moral Injury

Forgiveness is both especially important and especially challenging for those who suffer from moral injury. As we've noted, moral injury occurs under high-stakes circumstances where people's lives, relationships, and well-being are often at stake. You may find yourself thinking that forgiveness applies only to other people or for lesser violations. Perhaps the severity of the moral violation you experienced leads your mind to set it apart.

Certainly, the intensity of some moral violations may set them apart from more minor moral struggles (like telling "white" lies). But in another sense, it is essential to remember that you are still human (even if you have thoughts that you are not). You are still alive, so you must make choices about how you will live here and now. Forgiveness affords you an opportunity: the chance to (re)engage in values-consistent living.

If you do not entertain forgiveness, what is the path forward? And what does that path look like? Indeed, the stakes of being unforgiving are too high. The impact of perpetual punishment and refusal to forgive, on you and others you care for, may unwittingly continue to violate values—your values—and prevent healing and recovery for you and those connected to you. But healing can happen if you open yourself to approaching forgiveness as if it were an outward action.

Let's look at an example of forgiveness in action. A sixty-five-year-old veteran was seeking treatment for PTSD. He wasn't doing well; he was trapped in a habit of harsh self-criticism. He reported that one specific memory haunted him, but it was unlike the other traumatic memories he had worked on during treatment. While telling his story, he said that he had been a "coward" during the war and was ashamed that during a particular event he didn't take action to prevent a war crime.

As a soldier in Vietnam, this veteran had witnessed other soldiers desecrating the bodies of the enemy. Not only did these actions violate the rules of war established by the Geneva Convention, but the veteran also found them personally abhorrent and a violation of his own values. As the other soldiers engaged in this behavior, he stood by and watched. He was frozen in fear and took no action to stop them. He immediately felt ashamed, and as if he had behaved in a cowardly fashion for not stopping the soldiers. He felt the burden of the moral violation immediately, and he continued to carry it for the next forty-five years.

The veteran returned home from war, got married, and had children. He worked for many years but, plagued by PTSD and guilt, he eventually went on disability, staying at home most of the time and drinking. He withdrew from his wife and children for significant periods; at other times, he lashed out at them. He believed they should stay away from him. He worried they would see his cowardice and come to know him for "who he really was."

This veteran was suffering with moral injury. He was engaged in avoidance behaviors to try and suppress pain. He was absorbed by self-criticism and believed his mind when it said he didn't deserve to have good things in life, including his wife and children. He felt there was no punishment too great for his transgression and that a life of isolation was well deserved. He told his therapist that he could not forgive himself for what he had done. And yet, his value of integrity had not disappeared as a result of this violation. He still held it as a value, along with the values of being a good husband and father. Rather than trying to make him forget or rationalize his choices in war, therapy focused on forgiveness—the action.

Through learning to take different perspectives and exploring forgiveness in therapeutic sessions, the veteran realized that he was nineteen when the violation happened and that he was afraid to offend his fellow soldiers, whom he relied on for protection. Although this new understanding did not make him forget the event or justify his actions, by combining it with a willingness to feel his emotions and a desire to return to living with integrity, the veteran chose to give what came before. He began the process of forgiving himself by returning to living with integrity. The veteran imagined what the ideal outcome would be for that nineteen-year-old, had this moral violation not occurred. He then began to act in ways that were in line with that ideal. This included things like reaching out to his wife and children and working on connecting with them. It included reducing his isolation and alcohol use, and treating himself with more kindness. His work to forgive himself was a true act of courage.

Forgiveness in Relationship to Others: Reparations

Finally, consider the role of reparations in acts for forgiveness. Reparations are actions taken to make amends with those you may have hurt. In the past you may have considered offering such reparations to those you have trespassed against. If done in a spirit of openness, acknowledging and accepting the moral pain they are connected to, these activities are excellent ways to demonstrate values and can be undertaken in the service of self-forgiveness.

Reparations can come in all shapes and sizes; they can include anything from donating money to organizations to volunteering time for an important cause. They can consist of acts of kindness linked to values or concrete actions related to the moral violation itself. For instance, Robert might decide to volunteer for a children's organization, or the veteran might choose to help fellow veterans who have PTSD. Reparations can serve to honor values-based living and can build a personal future based on healing and recovery instead of punishment and pain.

As well, reparations often involve interactions with others, whether a group or an individual. They have social value, as they can build meaning rooted in past wrongs, even if the work of the repair isn't directly about the moral violation. Moral healing is about putting something that is torn or broken back together—specifically, relationships with the self and others. Reparations show others that a person is genuinely remorseful and willing to take action to heal a violation or wrong. This helps to restore trust in communities as well as trust in yourself. Being able to act in accordance with what matters most to you through amends is an act of love that creates a more positive relationship with yourself and betters your relationships with others.

Ultimately, the decision is yours, to engage in reparations or not. You may not feel ready for the activity of repair; you may not even think it necessary. You may not know where to begin. We offer the next exercise to help you explore the possibility.

Exercise 9.3: Considering Reparations

As you consider undertaking reparations, we invite you to work with kindness toward yourself as well as curiosity about the possibilities.

1. Based on your moral injury, have you ever considered making some repair as part of an act of forgiveness? If yes, why did you want to make that repair? If no, what would it mean to you to begin considering some repair?

_____

_____

_____

_____

_____

2. Do you think engaging in reparations would be useful for you and your healing? If yes, in what way? If no, what do you find challenging in thinking about reparations?

_____

_____

_____

3. If you were to make a repair, what would you choose to do? Take time and consider as many different activities as would make sense. Write two or three of them here.

_____

_____

_____

_____

_____

4. After you finish writing, reflect on the reparations process and consider whether it could be meaningful in terms of your moral healing. Would it have any meaning for you? If you find meaning in this process, consider taking action. Also, when you turn to chapter 11, consider whether one of your committed actions might be about reparations.

Heart and Mind: Living in Forgiveness

Have you ever had a sense of feeling truly free? If yes, remember the unencumbered feeling of that experience. Notice if you felt expansive, alive, and connected. We hope that you can experience that feeling again through the process of forgiveness. Forgiveness can free up space in your heart and mind, allowing you to grow in your empathy for yourself or others.

Withholding forgiveness can feed the emotions associated with the moral injury, discoloring how you see the world, relationships, and yourself. Unwillingness to forgive can negatively impact your future and change your perceptions of life as it is. Indeed, holding onto the pain can intensify your sorrow, leading to greater suffering, closing yourself off from feelings of being free. As we have noted, forgiveness does not erase the past; rather, it views what has happened in the past with empathy and compassion. It helps people rise above the fear and pain of moral violations. It doesn't change what has happened in the past but enlarges the possibilities for the future.

Exercise 9.4: You and Giving What Came Before

1.   Sit comfortably in a quiet place where you won't be disturbed. Take a few deep breaths, and gently close your eyes. Let yourself breathe naturally for a minute or two before you shift into the reflection.

2.   Now allow yourself to imagine that you have been forgiven—fully and wholly—for the moral violation that you are working on in this book. Imagine that you have forgiven yourself and that others have forgiven you, or imagine that you have fully forgiven others. Take time to notice what you experience when you consider this possibility.

3.   After imagining what it would be like if you were forgiven or forgave, open your eyes and write about your experience. Try not to retreat back into anger, or hatred. Simply let yourself stay with the possibility and write about how things might be.

_____

_____

_____

_____

_____

_____

_____

_____

We invite you to reflect on what you wrote and to fully consider making a difference for yourself by letting go of punishment and taking actions that give back to you and others the possibility of a more free, values-based life.

Summary

In this chapter, we explored what it means to *act* forgivingly rather than trying to *feel* forgiving or forgiven. Although you may feel a sense of relief or peace when working on forgiveness, these emotions are temporary and will rise and fall just like any other emotions. Forgiveness is about letting go of punishment and giving back to yourself or others what came before the moral violation—either the relationship you had with yourself or another, or something you hoped for in creating your life. The work of forgiveness can be challenging and may last for years, but the freedom from suffering and healing from pain you may gain is worth the time and effort. (For extra practice read and complete the worksheet A Bold Move of Forgiveness downloadable at http://www.newharbinger.com/44772.)

Forgiveness is intimately connected with compassionate practice. Compassion is a part of the work of forgiveness, and the subject we address in chapter 10.

Compassion: Cultivating Kindness and Connection

What is that one thing, which when you possess, you have all other virtues? It's compassion.

—Attributed to the Buddha

In chapter 9, we explored the role of forgiveness in moral injury. We also briefly introduced the idea of having compassion for oneself in the process of forgiveness and moral healing. Now we want to stretch into still more territory that is important, though perhaps not easy to explore. For those who experience moral injury, the work of compassion is particularly challenging. Many of us have the notion that compassion directed toward others or toward oneself is not deserved, especially for those who have violated values. However, we suggest that compassion is not only deserved, but essential.

We invite you to explore this chapter using much of what you have already learned from this book. We encourage you to read with an open, aware, and engaged stance, allowing what you feel, think, and sense to rise and fall as you stay committed to considering the benefits of compassion.

What Is Compassion?

What comes to mind when you think of the word "compassion" and its meaning? Take a moment to notice the thoughts, feelings, and sensations that show up when you consider this. Jot down your definition and the experiences you noticed when thinking about compassion.

_____

_____

_____

Each of us probably has a slightly different understanding of and relationship with compassion. Some may see compassion as a strength. Some may see it as a weakness. Some may see it as pity; others may see it as love. However you currently view compassion, it will be helpful to understand its true meaning. The definition of compassion is the felt sense that arises when we are confronted with suffering (that of others or our own) *and* feel an urge to alleviate or prevent that suffering.

In his book *CFT Made Simple: A Clinician's Guide to Practicing Compassion-Focused Therapy*, Dr. Russell Kolts (2016) says that "compassion is born of the recognition that, deep down, we all just want to be happy and don't want to suffer." He acknowledges that human life is hard. We struggle. And, in the face of struggle, if we evaluate ourselves as broken—isolating ourselves; criticizing, attacking, and rejecting ourselves and our pain—then we bring more suffering upon ourselves. However, responding to pain with compassion gives us an alternative, one that frees us to live our values more fully. The greater and more soul-wrenching the pain, the more compassion is needed.

In the face of moral injury, you have known great suffering. We invite you now to know great compassion.

Compassion After Trauma

Before we forge ahead, we want to share something with those who've experienced trauma—perhaps than more once—and have perhaps felt the need to stay strong and safe afterward. Some people who undergo trauma and hardship have developed a sense that compassion is for the weak, that it is a soft emotion. Others feel it is inappropriate, unwarranted, or undeserved. If you have felt this way, you are not alone.

In the face of traumatic events, wrongdoing, and seemingly inhuman behaviors, some people harden their hearts and steel their minds. They hope that hardening themselves will protect them from future trauma and future pain. It is not unusual to take this "better safe than sorry" approach. However, compassion has long been understood as one of the particularly well-developed strengths of sentient beings—the capacity to thrive and live with vitality in the midst of pain and vulnerability. To relinquish or reject this capacity deprives you of part of the essence of your humanity and a source of great strength. As such, we invite you to explore the value of compassion for moral healing.

Why Compassion for Moral Injury?

We can think of our emotions as an internal signaling system, telling us about events around us and in our relationships. These signals can inform us about possible choices we might make as we move forward in our actions, including those based in our values. Criticizing ourselves or others, blaming ourselves or others—all can interfere with this emotional capacity. Shutting down and isolating can also pull us away from what we care about most. Compassion can help to reverse these difficulties.

By building compassion, you can respond more quickly to yourself and others, and criticism and blame no longer need to be a barrier to vital living. Indeed, research on compassion-focused therapy (CFT) has shown the benefits of compassion, especially for those who are highly self-critical (Leaviss & Uttley, 2015; Luoma & Platt, 2015). The experience of compassion can motivate unselfish and thoughtful behavior. Through compassion, you can increase your caring for yourself and others, restoring relationships and community.

Ultimately, choosing to increase compassion toward yourself or others will be up to you. In making the choice, you might reflect on the costs of your self-criticism or criticism of others following the moral violation. You might also be curious about blame and how it has or has not served you. If you find that these are obstacles to your healing, then compassion may be part of what you need to move forward with your healing.

Exercise 10.1: The Critic, the Criticized Self, and the Compassionate Observer

This practice is adapted from a self-compassion exercise published by Dr. Kristin Neff (2009). Find a quiet place where you can do this exercise without interruption. You will be asked to consider three different aspects of yourself: (1) the critic, (2) the criticized self (the part of you that knows that you are being criticized and responds emotionally), and (3) the compassionate observer. It may be helpful to set up three different chairs you can sit in to help you "step into" each of these three senses of you. Or you can simply pretend to be in each role. You will write your reactions from the viewpoint of each one. The goal is to help you get in touch with these different parts of yourself and to notice what you experience as each.

1. To begin, you will assume the role (and chair) of the critic. Take a moment before you write to get in touch with your moral pain. Gently bring the memory of the experience to mind. Allow yourself to briefly visit the memory and its fallout without getting too caught up in the memory itself. Simply rest in the reflection for a few moments.

2. Begin to notice any criticisms that might arise as you consider the impact of the moral violation. Now let yourself step fully into the role of the critic—the part of you that evaluates and judges you for what happened. Say out loud what the critical part of you is thinking. For example, "I am unlovable because of what happened." "People will always betray me." "Forgiveness is out of reach." or "I am a horrible person." Express yourself honestly. Try to experience this aspect of yourself fully. As you speak as the critic, notice your thoughts, your tone of voice, your facial expressions, and your body language. Also notice which emotions are showing up.

3. Before you leave this role (chair), take a moment to describe your experience:

    a. What thoughts did the critic express?

    _____

    _____

    _____

    b. What was the critic's tone of voice?

    _____

    c. What facial expressions and body language does the critic have or do you imagine they might have?

    _____

    _____

4. Next, take the role (chair) of the criticized self. Imagine you are now hearing the critical thoughts just written by the critic, speaking with the tone and body language from that role. Picture yourself receiving the criticism.

5. From this perspective, say out loud the thoughts and feelings you experience in response to the words just shared by your inner critic. Respond directly to the critic; for example, "I feel hopeless when you say that." "That makes me incredibly sad." Express yourself honestly. Try to experience this aspect of yourself fully. Again, as you say these things, notice your words, tone of voice, facial expressions, and body language as well as the emotions that are showing up.

6. Take a moment to describe these experiences:

    a. What emotions did the criticized self have?

    _____

    _____

    _____

    b. What was the criticized self's tone of voice?

    _____

    c. What facial expressions and body language does the criticized self have or do you imagine they might have?

    _____

    _____

7. Next, step into the role (chair) of the compassionate observer. Anchor yourself in the present moment. You may want to imagine being someone you know who holds deep wisdom, caring concern, and kindness; however, it should still be a part of *you* sitting in this chair at this moment.

8. Imagine that you can see the critic and the criticized self in front of you. Allow yourself, as that compassionate observer, to first respond to the critic. You may wish to also speak these responses out loud before writing them down.

   a. What wisdom might you offer the critic in this moment as the compassionate observer?

   _____

   _____

   _____

   b. In this moment, how might you offer kindness to this critic?

   _____

   _____

   _____

9. Next, allow the compassionate observer to respond to the criticized self. Write your responses.

   a. What wisdom might you offer the criticized self?

   _____

   _____

   _____

   b. In this moment, how might you offer kindness to the criticized self?

   _____

   _____

   _____

Each of us holds each of these three aspects of self. Connecting to and understanding each of these parts of you—especially the compassionate observer—will help you to learn how to offer compassion to yourself and others. Remember from previous chapters that your true self is a stage that holds each of these selves, and that evaluation and judgment remove you from the present moment—the place where compassionate action happens. So when you notice your critic or criticized self showing up *or* when you notice others' critics or criticized selves joining the conversation, see if you can step back into that larger sense of self— that observing self who has an endless capacity to compassionately hold each of the different aspects of you.

Compassionate meditation—like the exercise you just completed—has been found to enhance well-being (Shonin, Van Gordon, Compare, Zangeneh, & Griffiths, 2015). The benefits of compassion include decreased emotional distress and improved mood, as well as increased positive thinking. Compassion also builds empathic accuracy, allowing you to better relate with others and their emotional responses. And, of course, compassion can improve relationships—which are often negatively impacted by moral injury and its fallout.

Understanding Compassion in Three Parts

Dr. Kristin Neff (2003), a prominent author and compassion researcher, says that self-compassion is composed of three parts: mindfulness, self-kindness, and common humanity. These components also comprise compassion for others (Pommier, 2011). Each of these parts of compassion is essential to building a compassionate stance toward yourself and others.

Mindfulness

In chapter 8, we focused on getting in touch with the present moment by paying attention to the here and now with mindful awareness or mindfulness. Mindfulness is paying attention with purpose; it requires a willingness to observe our thoughts, feelings, and sensations as well as our reactions to ourselves and others with openness and awareness in the present moment, without defense or judgment.

Mindfulness lays a foundation on which we can build the other compassion components. Mindful awareness allows us to experience uncomfortable, even painful, thoughts and emotions from a place of clarity and acceptance rather than confusion, conflict, or rejection. Rather than overly identifying with the past or negatively labeling yourself for the future, mindfulness allows you to observe what is here right now. It frees you up to engage in a way that decreases suffering and increases compassion.

By engaging in mindfulness, you build the capacity for greater emotional calmness and stability. You learn to respond to emotions with more ease and balance. This, in turn, affects the way you respond to others, reducing your reactivity to painful experiences like criticism, blame, shame, and anger. This allows you to engage in activities that invite connection and healing.

Kindness

Mindful awareness allows us choice. When we are aware, we better understand ourselves and our environment. We are not caught in thought and emotion, so we're free to see our way through to engage in actions consistent with our values. When you are mindful, you may still notice that the pain and deep ache of past mistakes, transgressions, or betrayals remain. At this choice point, compassion can represent the most helpful and healing response. Recall that compassion is the urge we feel to alleviate suffering and soothe pain when we observe it in ourselves or others. Kindness represents perhaps the best way to accomplish that goal.

Kindness is about being empathetic and gentle. It entails openness to and understanding of ourselves and others in the face of pain, failure, doubt, and difficulty. To be kind instead of critical in the face of pain is a powerful choice. And it is also a choice that can lessen the problem of ignoring, struggling against, or behaving harshly toward yourself or others because of the pain.

Kindness is *not* absolving yourself or others of actions for which you or they are responsible. Responsibility still remains, but how you take responsibility as you move forward matters. Choosing to live your values is part of that responsibility. Kindness is also *not* weakness, pity, or mere tolerance. Kindness is recognizing that pain is an inevitable part of human life. Indeed, it is a meaningful and vital part. Kindness is understanding that failure, even some of the most serious failures of our deepest values, is part of what it means to be human. Choosing kindness toward yourself and others as part of compassion is the path to learning, healing, growing, and reconnecting. When engaging in compassion, see if you can bring kindness to the work.

Acts of kindness may take many forms. These might include treating yourself to something you enjoy or spending time with loved ones. Showing compassionate kindness to others might include listening attentively while someone talks about their pain, or spending quality time together. For example, a solider with whom one of the authors worked felt betrayed by his unit and by army leadership. His act of kindness was to pray for the well-being of his unit and military leaders, even while requesting a transfer to a different unit. He did this because he felt that the best way he could extend compassion toward himself and toward the other soldiers by whom he felt betrayed was to move toward new relation-ships rather than continue to struggle against the current ones. This example shows that we can show compassionate kindness simultaneously to ourselves as well as to others.

Common Humanity

Perhaps the most essential component of compassion as it relates to moral injury is contacting and reconnecting with a shared sense of humanity. Remember, moral wounds are social wounds. These wounds are deeply cut, often creating a feeling that you are fully separated from others. To heal these wounds, it is important to acknowledge and embrace the commonalities of being human. You are not alone. *Common humanity,* as used in com-passionate practices, is the present-moment awareness that all humans experience pain, all humans fail, and—at one point or another—all humans suffer.

Social isolation—the opposite of connecting to that sense of common humanity—pre-vents moral healing. To isolate is to step away from others. This creates "aloneness" in suf-fering. It leads those engaged in isolation to feel that no one can understand or feel their pain. Moral injury in combination with isolation can make one almost feel nonhuman. Practicing compassion for self and others, recognizing that each human has their own measure of pain, decreases loneliness and supports connection to the community of humans who can help us regain our social standing and belonging.

Isolation is like putting a bandage over a very wide, jagged wound. The wound, while isolated, will not heal. In fact, it's likely to become infected, and the pain will increase. Getting stitches, instead, while painful and more difficult in some ways, brings the two sides of the wound back into contact where, with time and hard work (down to the cellular level), they can grow together again.

All humans have been wounded. And most, if not all, humans have been on both sides of a wounding (the wounded and the wounder). Contacting our common humanity in the present moment can help you both to feel less alone and also to experience greater empathy, kindness, and connection with others—others who love you and perhaps even others who have wronged you. When someone else's actions or inactions have harmed you, it may feel especially difficult to stay connected. Recognizing your common humanity and responding with kindness—whatever form that takes—will be a powerful and bold move toward healing.

Exercise 10.2: Compassion in a Simple Touch

For this exercise, sit in a quiet and comfortable place where you won't be disturbed for five to ten minutes.

1. Close your eyes as you reflect on your moral injury. Take just a few moments to gently observe the pain of this experience and how it has disconnected you from others and from your most authentic self.

2. Next, take a deep breath in and then, on the exhale, place your right hand over your heart and your left hand on top of the right hand. Take it slow. Then, breathing normally, simply begin to notice.

   a. Notice the sensations of your hand on your heart. Pause and observe.

   b. Notice the warmth flowing from your hand to your chest. Pause and observe.

   c. Notice the gentle pressure. Pause and observe.

   d. And, perhaps, notice a soothing sensation, peacefulness, or a sense of warmth and loving-kindness. Pause and observe.

3. Now, let's take it one step further. Through this hand placed just above your heart, send warmth, caring, and compassion into your chest. As if reaching out to a loved one in pain—a crying child, a whimpering pet, an ailing partner or parent—reach into yourself with this gentle but earnest desire to relieve suffering.

4. Continue noticing the sensations in the space where your hand contacts your chest. Notice if they change: relaxing, softening, warming. All the while, infuse soothing warmth and compassion, your heartfelt desire to be free of suffering. Spend as much time as you'd like here. There's no hurry and no limit to the amount of compassion you can send and receive.

What did you notice about the way this simple touch made you feel? Can you recall a time in your life when you felt a similar way? Maybe a tight hug from your caregiver as a child? A long embrace from your partner? Or holding your child for the first time? You can tap into this same process by compassionately connecting with yourself. A simple touch can be a great way to start: a warm hand over your heart is a simple and soothing way to offer yourself connection and compassion.

Cultivating Compassion for Moral Healing

Compassion flows in more than one direction: it flows from you to others and from others to you. So cultivating compassion in the service of healing from moral injury requires strengthening two skills: receiving compassion and practicing compassion.

Receiving compassion can be challenging. When you've experienced great pain, it can become quite difficult to openly receive compassion. It doesn't seem to fit with how you have come to understand yourself. It can feel foreign, strange, and undeserved. In these moments of compassion denial, remember the lessons of chapter 5. See if you can take a few steps back from these thoughts and allow the compassion to flow in around them.

Practicing compassion takes, well, practice. Continuing to work on being a compassionate observer of your experience takes effort and time. However, its soothing effect is worth it. Offering yourself kindness in a given moment and bringing to awareness the fact that you're not alone, that all humans suffer, will help you develop a sense of peace and wholeness—even if your pain stays with you. As well, compassion extended to others creates a soothing effect for them and fosters (re)connection. Reaching out in kindness will bring about healing and growth.

Summary

The practice of compassion is a deeply powerful and transformative experience. It may be among the greatest gifts you can offer yourself and others. As with most valuable skills, developing a compassionate posture toward yourself and others takes time and practice. There is a wealth of resources for learning more about compassion—how to know it and how to grow it. In this chapter, we have touched on only some basic elements of compassion and highlighted its important role in the moral healing process. (For extra practice read and complete the worksheet A Bold Move Toward Compassion downloadable at http://www .newharbinger.com/44772.)

Bishop Desmond Tutu once said, "Compassion is not just feeling with someone, but seeking to change the situation. Frequently people think compassion and love are merely sentimental. No! They are very demanding. If you are going to be compassionate, be prepared for action!" Compassion means taking action. That action is connecting to others in kindness and in the present moment. In the next and final chapter of this book, we'll invite you to stand and commit to bold actions in the service of vital living. Cultivating your compassion will be an essential bold move for healing from moral injury on your committed action journey.

CHAPTER 11

Living Is Doing

That which we persist in doing becomes easier—not that the nature of the task has changed, but our ability to do has increased.

—Ralph Waldo Emerson

We have come to the last chapter of this book, but not the last chapter of your journey. Indeed, we hope that your journey moving forward will be a new beginning. Opening this book, turning its pages, and exploring its message were preparation for the journey. But reading will never be enough. The words and exercises in these pages may bring insight and understanding, but to fulfill their promise, action is needed.

Action will mean taking risks. It will mean breaking out of old patterns. It will mean turning off the autopilot mode of doing and purposely focusing attention on what is in front of you here and now. Action is about choosing to do something based on your personally held values, and then following through with footsteps that bring that action to life.

Footsteps matter here. Breaking free from your suffering with moral injury is more about moving your feet than about moving your mind. This is because vitality in life will never be lived in the mind alone. We know this because our attempts to find vitality by fixing our minds have only increased our suffering. Vitality does not come from thinking; vitality happens only by doing. And then by doing again, and again, and again. Each action requires conscious choice. Step by step, each day is a new journey, defined by your values.

Healing from Moral Injury: Committed Action

In chapter 2, we introduced you to the core processes of ACT. One of those processes was *committed action*, the focus of this final chapter. *Committed action* is the ongoing and active engagement in values-aligned behavior. Let's take a closer look at what is meant by this process.

The Latin origin of the word *committed* is a combination of two words: *com*, meaning "together," and *mittere*, meaning "to send." It indicates a binding of a person and their intention as they are sent forward in life. Thus, in taking a committed action, a person is bound to a chosen value as they take each step of their journey. If values function as the compass, guiding our direction, then committed actions are the means by which we move forward on the journey.

Getting Unstuck

Moral injury carries a high cost with respect to your relationships, your sense of self, and your ability to engage meaningfully in the world. The moral violation itself emerged from events or actions that were inconsistent with your values. The moral injury flowed out of your sincere attempts to avoid or somehow control the fallout—pain, guilt, shame, anger—of this violation. However, your attempts to control the pain have exacted ever higher costs in terms of quality of life.

Life's possibilities become smaller and smaller in the face of moral injury and the effort to avoid its emotional effects. This effort to avoid is like being on a bicycle with a broken chain—you can pedal as fast as you want, but the bike goes nowhere. You make a tremendous effort, but you remain stuck. Committed action is about reattaching the bike chain. Reconnecting to your values and bringing them to life through your behavior—pedaling with purpose—starts you moving again and in a direction that matters to you most.

Exercise 11.1: Reflections on Avoidance

Think back to when you first began reading this book. Take time to reflect on what you were feeling, thinking, and sensing as you began to read. Were you hopeful—or doubtful? Did you expect that reading this book would resolve your emotional experience or make the pain go away? Notice whether there has been a shift as you have continued to read. Can you see now that avoidance is no longer the solution? Write about your reflections:

_____

_____

_____

_____

_____

Committed action is about letting go of ineffective control. Certainly some forms of control can be helpful and enhance your values. However, controlling through avoidance often robs you of those opportunities. Staying away from what you feel and think becomes the dictator of your actions. Values-based steps make meaningful movement possible again.

Committed Action: Living Values, Taking Risks

Recall in chapter 6 that we explored values and moral pain as two sides of the same coin. Values and pain are inseparable. You experience moral pain linked to the morally injurious experience because an important value was violated. Now, whenever you pursue that value, your moral pain will tend to make itself known. Pursuing your values through committed actions means being willing to have that pain reemerge into your awareness. The invitation to hold this pain as you move forward isn't about feeling it for its own sake; rather, it is about feeling it in the service of once again living your values.

Imagine a foreign city that you've always wanted to explore. For years you looked at pictures and read stories about the history of this wonderful place. You dreamed of visiting it one day, so you began to save. Finally, you were able to go. When you arrived, you decided that the best way to see the whole city was to take a hop-on hop-off double-decker tour bus. You buy the ticket and wait in line to board the bus. You suddenly feel anxious and doubtful—a feeling you have felt before. Suddenly you are wondering if you should get on the bus. You ask yourself: _Is it the right one? Will I like the tour? Who are these people standing in line? Should I wait? Maybe another bus would be better. Have I made the right decision? What should I do?_

This "board the bus" scenario epitomizes both the dilemma and the simplicity of committed action. Once you've identified an important value (perhaps the very value that was violated in the morally injurious experience), as well as an action that supports that value, truly nothing could be simpler. Simply take the action. Commit and step forward. There is risk; we don't always know the outcome (what if it's the wrong bus?), but not stepping at all is far more costly.

On the imaginary bus tour, this means that when the bus door opens, you take a step up and into the bus. Taking that step is a committed act. It moves you forward in the values-based adventure. Yet in this scenario, it means also being accompanied by whatever discomfort is present. Anxiety and doubt come along for the trip. Your values, not your emotions and thoughts, are guiding your actions.

Reflecting again on your moral injury, consider what experiences might need to come along for the ride. Will you willingly be present to these experiences and step forward?

Exercise 11.2: Identify a Bold Move

If you've worked through this book in a systematic way, you've already identified an event that has generated significant moral pain for you. You've also likely identified the value that's on the flip side of that pain.

1. In the Bold Move table following on the lines in column 1, take a moment to write one or more of the values that were violated.

2. For column 2, take some time to think about what past actions you've engaged in in your efforts to avoid your moral pain, control it, or push it away. Write these down as well.

3. In column 3, list several actions you could take *today* that would give expression to your important value that was violated (the value in column 1). These actions can take many forms. They can be small or large, but they need to be something you could do today—even, right now, if you were to set aside this book.

4. In column 4, list what has gotten in your way until now and prevented you from taking action.

5. Now for the most important part of this exercise. Pick one of the actions you listed in column 3 and do it—today. Don't let anything in column 2 take over, and don't let column 4 stop you. Bring any thoughts and feelings along for the ride. Find one that is doable now, and take action.

Table 11.1: Bold Move

1. Value(s) violated in the morally injurious event	2. What I've done to avoid the moral pain that followed the event	3. Actions I can take that express the values in column 1	4. What might seem to get in the way (thoughts, feelings, sensations)?

6. After completing the Bold Move table, take some time to reflect on the action you took. What thoughts and feelings came up before you acted? What did you experience afterward? Remember to always have compassion, no matter what you experienced.

Living a vital and meaningful life means taking actions that breathe life into our most important values. One way to begin to do this is by identifying bold moves that you can do every day, building new patterns of behavior over time that create your meaning.

Obstacles to Committed Action

Living your most important values with every step isn't easy. Think about how, at the beginning of each year, people make New Year's resolutions; then, in the days and weeks that follow, the resolutions often fade away. What happens? What goes wrong when people set out to make a change and later realize that they are back in old patterns of behavior? We surmise that although they are eager for the outcome, they have forgotten that life is a process. Values-based living is never something we achieve once and for all; rather, it's about engaging in those meaningful actions again and again and again.

It takes persistence to continue engaging in action from a firm stance of willingness. It takes persistence to stick with a course of action despite difficulty or opposition. Now, being persistent doesn't mean being inflexible—there are many ways to live a value. But persistent action is required to achieve goals related to purposeful living.

So what gets in the way? What interferes with persistence?

Avoidance or Being Unwilling to Feel

Any number of obstacles will emerge when we seek to persist in committed actions. In the context of moral injury, unwillingness to feel can be an intense obstacle, seeming to block your path forward. Indeed, in choosing to pursue an action that is consistent with the value that was violated during the moral injury, you may begin to think about the event and experience some of its related emotions such as anger, guilt, and shame. You may feel these intensely, even viscerally. Your wish to avoid these experiences makes intuitive sense, but turning away from the emotions also means turning away from the committed action. If you surrender to this impulse of avoidance, stuckness is sure to follow.

Turning away from pain keeps you tied to the past because you must "touch" the past in order to know to avoid the pain. It does take courage to turn toward your pain. It takes willingness to feel whatever emotions and sensations will rise and fall when you do so. But as you persist, stepping forward with actions consistent with your values, you will open yourself to the possibility of new experiences—and with them, new and different emotions and thoughts.

Some avoidance tactics, such as alcohol abuse or isolation, are obvious, but others are more subtle. We may be avoiding when we engage in behaviors that are not normally problematic but make it more difficult to follow through with our commitments. To better understand how this kind of subtle avoidance can serve as an obstacle in the context of moral injury, let's return to the story of Robert, introduced in chapter 1, whose son was killed in a car accident.

Before the accident, Robert was working multiple jobs to help keep the family financially intact. Would it be surprising that, after the accident, being around his family might be painful? Robert might make a choice to "take care of his family" by working even more hours. While this might fulfill one aspect of taking care of his family, it might also serve as an avoidance tactic, preventing him from being physically present with his wife and child in their time of need.

Being consciously aware of your motives can help you overcome both obvious and more subtle avoidance tactics. For Robert, choosing to persist in his values of caring and love might mean being with his family even while carrying his pain.

In addition to experiencing intense emotions, you may struggle with strong evaluative thoughts. Fusing with these thoughts can also lead to being stuck. Getting lost in such thoughts, pulling you back into the past, presents another barrier to healing.

Getting Absorbed in or "Buying" Your Thoughts

Most people would have difficulty even imagining the emotional pain of Robert's loss or the moral pain of feeling responsible for it. The value that Robert felt he had violated was that of caring for and protecting his children. Imagine his difficulty even looking at his remaining child and his wife, and imagine the intensely powerful guilt and shame that might arise in their presence. You can almost hear the condemning thoughts that his mind would produce: *You should've died yourself. You don't deserve to have a family after what you did. You are a terrible person for looking at a text while driving! There is something wrong with you.* Would you be surprised if, in the grip of his intense moral pain, Robert chose to avoid those painful moments by distancing himself from his family or drinking?

What would committed action, directed toward the value that was violated in this event, look like? What would be required to live out the value of caring for and protecting his family in this present moment? First, if Robert chose to engage the values that were violated, he would likely experience the thoughts just suggested. Defusing from these thoughts would help him to persist. He could see these thoughts as just that—thoughts—and recognize that he is more than any of these thoughts.

Second, he could spend time with his family in the midst of their shared pain of loss, rather than pulling away and distancing himself. Committed action would likely also involve reengaging in the same activities he used to do with both children and now can continue to do with the child who remains. This might include simple things like helping with homework or going out for ice cream. Being willing, in the face of strong and painful emotions, to be present to love and care for his remaining child would also be considered committed action.

Mindless Living

A final obstacle to committed action may be the lure of living without awareness. Throughout this book we've described mindfulness as "paying attention, on purpose, in the present moment, without judgment" (Kabat-Zinn, 2009). We have encouraged you to practice mindfulness as a way to be more fully present to the moment and your life. This is also a key part of engaging compassion. Practicing mindfulness is an essential way to develop the skill of noticing. We often fall out of touch with noticing due to our busy minds. This causes problems in living in the moment and in choosing actions according to our values.

Let's explore a quick example. One amazing but challenging thing about the human brain is its ability to perform certain tasks of daily living in the background, without our having to think much about them. Remember when you first learned to drive? You had to give your full attention to everything you did and everything around you—it was a matter of survival! You were intensely aware of pressing the gas pedal or the brake. You were aware of steering the car and staying in the lane. You drove with absolute focus. Chances are, though, that as you've gained experience your level of awareness while driving has diminished. You now experience driving differently. You can think and talk and do other things while driving. This is fine most of the time. But sometimes we become completely unaware while driving and miss our exit, or arrive somewhere with no recollection of how we got there. Failing to pay full attention can lead to difficulties. It can also lead to danger.

Similarly, in life, failing to take time to notice what's present around us and within us can also keep us from living our most important values. There are a multitude of activities that can fill up our lives, many of which have the potential to pull us into mindless living. We often mechanically move through the day without noticing the here and now. Time passes, and that which is most important to us slips away. Mindful living means regularly noticing where you are at and where you are headed.

We can also find meaning and purpose through engaging in activities that matter because they reflect our deepest values. Prioritizing these important activities in the moment is the stuff of values-based living and can bring us more joy and vitality. We cannot choose these activities, however, if we move through life unaware. There is a fitting quote attributed to President Dwight Eisenhower that expresses this idea: "What is important is seldom urgent, and what is urgent is seldom important."

Jump!

The word "jump" means "to spring free from the ground or other base by the muscular action of feet and legs." A person can jump in any direction: forward, backward, or to the side. Jumping is an action. *Thinking* about jumping is not jumping. *Planning* to jump is not jumping. Only *jumping* is jumping. And once we jump, there's no turning back. Gravity is in charge until we land. To jump is a choice. One can jump at any moment, or not.

Committed action is like jumping. Once we let our values set the direction, all that's left to do is jump.

When you jump, it's not that a part of you jumps. Your whole self goes with you. You jump with your thoughts, feelings, and sensations. When you spring into the air, all that you are comes along.

This is the simplicity of committed action. Jump or don't jump—life will unfold accordingly. To promote your own moral healing, to reclaim sources of meaning and purpose in life, to renew sources of power and intention within yourself…we invite you to jump.

Exercise 11.3: A Final Exercise: Living Well

In this last exercise, we invite you to reflect on the journey of exploring the work in this book. Take time to reflect and write about what you have learned or what struck you as most important. Write about your journey here:

_____

_____

_____

_____

_____

_____

_____

_____

Next, we invite you to set some values-based intentions. What actions will you take? And how will you do it? Describe them here:

My values-based intentions are:

_____

_____

I will live these intentions by taking these specific actions:

_____

_____

(For extra practice read and complete the worksheet Turning Values into Actions downloadable at http://www.newharbinger.com/44772.)

Conclusion

As we reach the end of the journey of this book, and you continue the journey of healing from moral injury, we express our hopes for you and your ability to live well. Healing from moral injury means opening up to joy *and* pain, defusing from unhelpful thoughts, living more fully in the here and now, and connecting to a sense of yourself that is much more than your emotions, thinking, memory, and moral pain. You'll find your path to a meaningful and purpose-filled life by working on forgiveness and compassion, turning more fully to living a values-based life, and persisting in committed actions. We wish you well on this journey.

References

Davis, D. M., & Hayes, J. A. (2011). What are the benefits of mindfulness? A practice review of psychotherapy-related research. *Psychotherapy, 48*(2), 198–208. doi.org /10.1037 /a0022062

Haidt, J. (2001). The emotional dog and its rational tail: A social intuitionist approach to moral judgment. *Psychological Review, 108*(4), 814–834. doi.org /10.1037/033-295X.108 .4.814

Hayes, S. C., Strosahl, K. D., & Wilson, K. G. (2012). *Acceptance and commitment therapy: The process and practice of mindful change,* 2nd ed. New York, NY: Guilford Press.

Kabat-Zinn, J. (2009). *Letting everything become your teacher: 100 lessons in mindfulness.* New York, NY: Random House Publishing.

Kohlberg, L. (1981). *The philosophy of moral development: Moral stages and the idea of justice.* San Francisco: Harper & Row.

Kolts, R. L. (2016). *CFT made simple: A clinician's guide to practicing compassion-focused therapy.* Oakland, CA: New Harbinger Publications.

Kuhn, M. H., & McPartland, T. S. (1954). An empirical investigation of self-attitudes. *American Sociological Review, 19,* 68–76. doi.org/10.2307/2088175

Leaviss, J., & Uttley, L. (2015). Psychotherapeutic benefits of compassion-focused therapy: An early systematic review. *Psychological Medicine, 45*(5), 927–945. doi.org/10.1017/S00 33291714002141

Luoma, J. B., & Platt, M. G. (2015). Shame, self-critism, self-stigma, and compassion in Acceptance and Commitment Therapy. *Current opinion in psychology, 2,* 97–101.

Neff, K. (2003). Self-compassion: An alternative conceptualization of a healthy attitude toward oneself. *Self and Identity, 2,* 85–101. doi.org/10.1080/15298860309032

Neff, K. (2009). Self-compassion exercises: Exercise 3. Retrieved from https://www.mcgill.ca /counselling/files/counselling/self-compassion_exercises_0.doc

Pommier, E.A. (2011). The compassion scale. *Dissertation Abstracts International Section A: Humanities and Social Sciences, 72*(4-1), 1174. Retrieved from https://self-compassion.org /wp-content/uploads/2015/03/CompassionScale-8.doc

Shonin, E., Van Gordon, W., Compare, A., Zangeneh, M., & Griffiths, M. D. (2015). Buddhist-derived loving-kindness and compassion meditation for the treatment of psychopathology: A systematic review. *Mindfulness, 6*(5), 1161–1180. doi.org/10.1007/s126 71-014-0368-1

Walser, R. D., & Westrup, D. (2007). *Acceptance and commitment therapy for the treatment of post-traumatic stress disorder and trauma-related problems: A practitioner's guide to using mindfulness and acceptance strategies.* Oakland, CA: New Harbinger Publications.

Wilson, K. G., & DuFrene, M. T. (2008). *Mindfulness for two: An acceptance and commitment therapy approach to mindfulness in psychotherapy.* Oakland, CA: New Harbinger Publications.

Wyatt R. Evans, PhD, is a board-certified clinical psychologist with the VA North Texas Health Care System, and therapist in private practice in the Dallas-Fort Worth area. His primary areas of expertise are resilience and post-traumatic stress, including moral injury. He is committed to advancing interventions, especially acceptance and commitment therapy (ACT), to promote recovery and enhance resilience for service members, veterans, and others highly affected by trauma.

Robyn D. Walser, PhD, is director of TL Consultation Services, codirector of the Bay Area Trauma Recovery Clinic, staff at the National Center for PTSD, and an associate clinical professor at the University of California, Berkeley. As a licensed clinical psychologist, she maintains an international training, consulting, and therapy practice. She is an expert in ACT, has coauthored six books on the subject, and is author of *The Heart of ACT*.

Kent D. Drescher, PhD, is a clinical psychologist (retired) who provided clinical services, education, and research as a staff member with the National Center for PTSD for more than twenty-seven years. His primary areas of expertise include the intersection of trauma and spirituality and moral injury. He has been an early advocate for the use of ACT for veterans struggling with moral challenges following military service.

Jacob K. Farnsworth, PhD, is a licensed clinical psychologist with the VA Eastern Colorado Health Care System, specializing in trauma and substance use disorders. He is codeveloper of the ACT for moral injury intervention, and his writing and research has focused on translating cutting-edge research into innovative and effective treatments for moral injury.

Real change *is* possible

For more than forty-five years, New Harbinger has published proven-effective self-help books and pioneering workbooks to help readers of all ages and backgrounds improve mental health and well-being, and achieve lasting personal growth. In addition, our spirituality books offer profound guidance for deepening awareness and cultivating healing, self-discovery, and fulfillment.

Founded by psychologist Matthew McKay and Patrick Fanning, New Harbinger is proud to be an independent, employee-owned company. Our books reflect our core values of integrity, innovation, commitment, sustainability, compassion, and trust. Written by leaders in the field and recommended by therapists worldwide, New Harbinger books are practical, accessible, and provide real tools for real change.

 **newharbinger**publications

MORE BOOKS *from*
NEW HARBINGER PUBLICATIONS

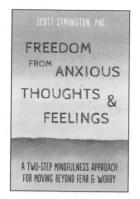
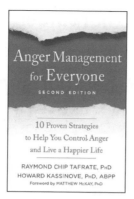
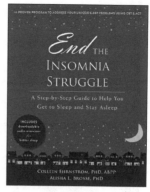
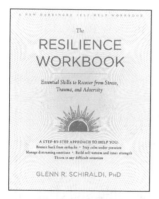

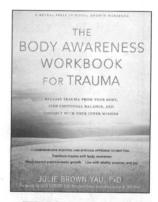

Register your **new harbinger** titles for additional benefits!

When you register your **new harbinger** title—purchased in any format, from any source—you get access to benefits like the following:

- Downloadable accessories like printable worksheets and extra content
- Instructional videos and audio files
- Information about updates, corrections, and new editions

Not every title has accessories, but we're adding new material all the time.

Access free accessories in 3 easy steps:

1. Sign in at NewHarbinger.com (or **register** to create an account).

2. Click on **register a book**. Search for your title and click the **register** button when it appears.

3. Click on the **book cover or title** to go to its details page. Click on **accessories** to view and access files.

That's all there is to it!

If you need help, visit:

NewHarbinger.com/accessories

new harbinger
CELEBRATING
40 YEARS